A BETTER VOICE

STRAIGHT FROM THE ENTERTAINMENT INDUSTRY FRONTLINES

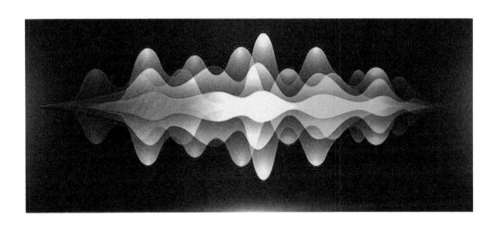

Valerie Morehouse

© Valerie Morehouse 2023
valerie@valeriemorehouse.com

Interior format and cover design by Dorothy Dreyer
Published by The Book Hub Publishing Group with
offices in Galway and Limerick, Ireland
www.bookhubpublishing.com

Print ISBN: 978-1-7392899-7-3

*Book Hub Publishing is committed to inclusion and
diversity. We use paper sourced from sustainable
forestry and are committed to the protection of our
global environment.

TABLE OF CONTENTS

A BETTER VOICE

STRAIGHT FROM THE ENTERTAINMENT INDUSTRY FRONTLINES

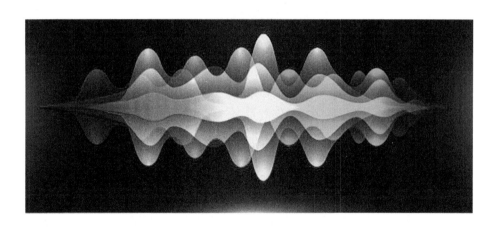

Valerie Morehouse

© Valerie Morehouse 2023
valerie@valeriemorehouse.com

Interior format and cover design by Dorothy Dreyer
Published by The Book Hub Publishing Group with
offices in Galway and Limerick, Ireland
www.bookhubpublishing.com

Print ISBN: 978-1-7392899-7-3

*Book Hub Publishing is committed to inclusion and
diversity. We use paper sourced from sustainable
forestry and are committed to the protection of our
global environment.

TABLE OF CONTENTS

GRATITUDE FOR
A BETTER VOICE"

"Singers are by nature, very vulnerable. Finding someone who can communicate with them in a language they can understand, give them techniques they can employ that improves their performance immediately, and above all, instill confidence in them to go out and do their job more effectively, is a rare commodity. Val is that rare commodity...She is simply the best."

—Jay DeMarcus, *Rascal Flatts*

"In all of my years as a professional singer, I have never had an experience with a vocal trainer who not only understood the technical science behind what helps maintain a strong singing voice, but those factors of speaking and life stresses that can cause vocal fatigue. Valerie has taught me how to recognize a problem and work around it without causing damage to my voice when dealing with a heavy touring schedule. I notice an immediate improvement after every session."

—Noelle Scaggs, *Fitz and the Tantrums*

"Val is as real as they come. I've been lucky enough to work with her since I was fifteen years old. All of the progress I've made has been down to her love, support, and encouragement, to help me see and believe in myself."

—Noah Cyrus, Singer/Actor

"The exercise and vocal tips Valerie has given me have made singing more fun, more relaxed. Her scientific and personal approach really worked for me. She's taught me ways of using my voice that have helped my pitch, phrasing and clarity, without altering my personal style. She's really turned me on to the joy of singing."

—Jeff Bridges, Actor

"I was lucky enough to find Valerie while I was dealing with a paralyzed vocal cord in 2011. Not only did I find someone to help me retrain what I was left with to broadcast games, I also found a friend. She is tireless with what she does for a living, and I get the sense she would do it for free. Training voices, singing and speaking, are her vocation and her avocation. That's special."

—Joe Buck, Sportscaster

"Val always brings a great energy and vibe into the working atmosphere. She has incredible understanding and a bank of knowledge that's always very motivating and inspiring."

—Matt McGuire, *The Chainsmokers,* Drummer/Music Director

"Valerie has been my singing teacher for six years, in-between film projects. Not only has she helped me learn how to use the instrument I have, but Val gives me more confidence in my music and in myself as an artist, to land the film roles and achieve more goals in my life."

—Ruby Rose, Actor/Singer

"Were it not for my on-going training, I never would be sustaining a public career that has lasted over thirty-five years! For me, it's a rare day when I can wake up and accidentally sing to my fullest potential. It's all about Val's training and technique!"

—Debbie Gibson, Singer/Recording Artist

"Val is the essence of a true master of her craft. It has been an honor to be her student."

—Calum Hood, *Five Seconds of Summer,* Bassist/Vocalist

"Learning about my voice is something I've always been very insecure about. Val's approach is so empowering, in that the more you know, the more you can feel confident about using the most personal and emotive instrument you have. It's changed my perspective entirely."

—Hunter Hayes, Singer/Recording Artist

"With the demands placed on a modern artist, it's more important than ever to have a knowledgeable, invested vocal coach. That is exactly who Val is. The rigors of touring, recording, press appearances, etc, can take an immense, physical toll. Valerie appreciates the mechanics behind the instrument, and holds the tools to elevate and sustain an artist's most critical asset, the voice."

—Stacy Jones, Drummer and MD for Miley Cyrus
Olivia Rodrigo, Drummer and Performer

"As a half-deaf singer, I have had my share of challenges. You can't sing what you can't hear. Two things have presented me with the voice I used to wistfully hear in my dreams; digital hearing aids and Valerie Morehouse. Val's gift for training the technical aspects of the voice includes the ability to reach beyond my hearing disability, helping me to sense where I need to be. Val gives me the tools to consistently find the correct connection and resonance, never allowing me to give up or think less of myself as a performer with additional needs. Finding my voice and stepping out of silence and isolation is my soul's path at its center, and Val has always honored this journey as sacred."

—Elizabeth W. Krasnoff, PhD
Sound Medicine

"I've worked with many, many vocal coaches in my career, but I've never seen anyone pay the kind of attention to detail as Valerie. Her techniques make the best singers even better, and the ones who dream of becoming professional singers someday... she actually helps make those dreams a reality!"

—Rodney Jerkins, Record Producer; Songwriter;
Rapper; Record Executive

"Before working with Val, my voice would 'go out' all the time on tour. It was really hard to keep up night after night. Working with Val has taught me healthy placement, transforming my live performances forever. Her technique is unmatched and I'm so grateful for everything she has shown me."

—Kim Petras, Singer/Recording Artist

"A great teacher reveals a deeper part of you that hasn't yet been touched upon. My time with Valerie not only revealed that I had better pipes than I once thought, but through her exercises, I discovered a more focused, aware and determined part of me which has been of service ever since. And...
It was SUCH FUN to spend time with her in the sandbox of her skill sets! I cherish that time, golden and full of love, so much so that we have remained friends ever since. My time with Valerie Morehouse was invaluable."

—Josh Brolin/Actor

FOREWORD SECTION

"In November of 2006, six months after signing with Jimmy Lovine and Interscope Records, I stepped into the studio of Valerie Morehouse for the first time. I had been referred to her by a Los Angeles ENT after a particularly rigorous few months of touring. As a member of both the head-lining band, as well as front-man of the opening act on that tour, I was performing ten shows per week, and spending my days *off* in the studio, laying the groundwork for what would become our major label debut.

As the son of two singer/songwriter children of the sixties, I grew up singing jingles for my dad, and in church, singing with my mother on the week-ends. Having been reared with a fascination and reverence for vocal titans, the likes of Edgar Winter, Freddie Mercury and Bobby McFerrin, from a young age I was keenly aware of the concept of the human voice as an instrument. Later shifting my focus to guitar and song-writing in my adolescence, I began to approach singing more as a story-telling tool, as well as a vehicle by which a song might be transported.

With the singularity of voice and rawness of acts such as The Beatles, The Beach Boys, and B.B. King, among my musical guiding lights, I was hesitant to allow anything overtly technical to pose a hinderance to my creative mission…with the assumption that any form of conscious vocal training might seek to homogenize that singularity of voice we all, as artists, seek to realize. This is the frame of mind with which my very first warm-up with Valerie was met, on that Autumn Day in 2006…

I expressed these concerns to Valerie, as I express them here, now. And after that first, nearly hour-long session, I walked away feeling no more convinced that a curriculum in proper vocal technique would be the movement most in line with my personal goal as a singer and as an artist. So much so, that it would be another fourteen months before I would contact her again for a follow-up lesson.

January 22, 2008…I remember the day as many remember days of great tragedy in the course of human existence. The news was breaking through-out the morning of the untimely passing of another hero of mine, Heath Ledger. Having never met him, I felt unusually saddened by the impact of this passing of a man who, apart from our communion through celluloid, would otherwise be considered a stranger. But I had admired his work, and had been inspired by his spirit, and his dedication to his craft.

And the voice doesn't lie.

As actors and musicians, we use our voices to tell the truth, oftentimes revealing ourselves behind a mask. Call it metaphysical, psychological, or a unique confluence of the two, the expression of the human voice is not purely physical. The revelation of one's true voice is an experience of the mind, body and spirit. I believe that our bodies function in a similar manner. And on that day, I came down with the kind of respiratory infection we, as humans, are well acquainted with, but one most wouldn't need attempt sing through. I, however, had a sold-out show at The Troubador that coming Saturday night, our first at the venue, and now, mere days away, vocal phonation was nevertheless unmoved by the five hundred tickets we had sold to those expecting a really great show on Santa Monica Boulevard that evening.

Having exhausted the options of chamomile tea with honey and lemon, steamers, throat coat and lozenges, I reticently reached for the recording I had made of my very first lesson with Valerie, on that Autumn Day, two years prior. I sang one of the best shows I had sung to date, that L.A. winter evening at The Troubador, and the very next week, I found myself back in Valerie's studio, ready to absorb any knowledge she would be inspired to share.

It's been that way ever since.

Over three hundred and fifty lessons later, two thousand plus performances on Broadway, including many musical trips around the world, I find myself returning to Valerie's studio, each conversation, each warm-up, un-locking something new in this joyous, unending quest of understanding the human voice."

—Reeve Carney, Singer/ Actor

"Singing, to me, is one of the greatest tools we have. If you look back in history, singing has been used to make people feel better throughout some of the world's most traumatic and awful times.
I have always been drawn to singing, ever since childhood. I simply loved the way it felt...I still do. The actual *feeling* that accompanies singing is something I adore.

I remember the first time, however, that I truly faced trouble with my voice. I was fourteen, and due to perform in front of my entire school. I was warmed-up and prepared for the performance, my voice feeling strong; better than ever... but all of a sudden, I found myself extremely scared. When I opened my mouth to sing, the sound that came out sounded nothing like it had only ten minutes before I went on stage. I was confused, very upset and completely at a loss as to what was going on.

It was that day, that performance, when I first realized the direct correlation between the voice as a physical instrument, and how we are *feeling* in the moments we are using it. Our moods and emotions are equally as important as the health of the anatomy of the voice and the sounds it can produce.

The only way to override the emotions when singing, is through training. I remember first hearing that Stevie Wonder **still** trains every single day. When I discovered this, I knew that *proper* training was going to be part of my life forever.

I am human, as are you. Things happen in our lives that sometimes inhibit our ability to look after our voices. I am so fortunate to have a teacher who allows me to be open and honest, understanding me as I continue to learn to understand myself. She works alongside me as my life and career continue to unfold. This brings me to Valerie.

Valerie is honestly the most incredible teacher I've ever had. She has shown me pathways with my voice that I didn't even know were available. Val has brought my attention to the gift we have as singers, how to look after that gift, and make the most out of it when sharing it with others.

Recently, I gave my first performance on stage in four years. That final performance, four years prior, I was racked with nerves, my throat closed up and I was left feeling utterly helpless. As my return to the stage grew closer, I was beyond nervous that this would happen to me again.

I made a decision, however, to step up my training before the show, and really focus on my instrument and how I was feeling about it. As Valerie puts it, I was *"becoming bulletproof"*.

When I stepped on that stage not so long ago, I felt grounded; completely centered and held to the floor, both emotionally and spiritually. For the first time in such a long time, I was able to enjoy and share my gift simultaneously. I wasn't working, I wasn't even singing...

I was gliding.

I never thought that was possible. I had heard other singers explain the feeling, but with all of the stresses and pressures imposed by a pop music career, *gliding* through a performance was nothing but a myth to me.

I now know it to be true. I now understand that with training and focus that is anchored in tender love and care, as well as good, honest guidance, the sky's the limit when it comes to the potential of the voice.

This book is a blessing to singers and performers alike. I hope you will find the help you need within, just as I have.
Keep singing your heart out and when in need, know that Valerie is the singer's friend. A true friend!

The wisdom that has changed many careers and lives, including my own, is now accessible to us all."

—Sam Smith, Singer/Recording Artist

"I met Valerie Morehouse in 2011, one week after I had surgery on my vocal cords. I came to her with only a tiny bit of hope that I could sing or speak again. I had no idea Valerie and her technique were going to change my life, as well as my career. The way that Valerie taught me to sing correctly, along with strengthening my vocal cords and voice, was not something I had ever experienced before. Prior to working with Valerie, I had been forced to cancel so many shows, however, since 2011, I have not cancelled a single performance. She is kind, brilliant, passionate, and helpful in every way. Since working with Valerie, I have fallen so madly in love with vocal health and her techniques, that I try to share this knowledge with every singer I come in contact with. I could never thank Valerie enough for the strength and confidence she has instilled in me as a singer. Everyone I know should read this book, take the time to learn about their voice and sing out big, bright, and healthy."

—Christina Perri, Singer/Recording Artist

♪ A Note From The Editor ♪

On a beautiful and balmy California morning five years ago, I eagerly sat as a visitor in the audience of a monthly breakfast club' for major players in the Los Angeles music industry. The sun danced across the lapping waves of the Pacific, just outside the picture windows of a beach-front venue in Malibu. The main speaker took to the stage with a blend of humility and confidence that had my full attention before a single word was even spoken. She was mesmerizing and elegantly accessible, as she presented her ground-breaking work in vocal training, dropping the jaws of the most seasoned and successful producers and musicians in the room.

After the event, we were all invited to the home and state-of- the-art studio of an award-winning music producer. I remember standing outside, looking out over the water, scarcely able to believe that a small-town doc from the middle of Ireland was surrounded by folks who had created some of my favorite music and scored some of the block-buster films which had captured my heart, immersing me in the stories through perfectly appointed sounds.

This was the setting in which I first met Valerie Morehouse. It was one of those moments... you know the kind. When kindred spirits cross paths and there is a 'knowing', that a new chapter, a deep and meaningful relationship has just begun. We weren't long in conversation when the topic of writing came up. I had to ask...

"Have you considered writing a book? Your experiences, your knowledge, this incredibly unique technique you have created… people need to know this!"

I was delighted to hear that Val had a vast amount of content already written, tucked away for the right moment. *This was that moment.*

As a Doctor of Chiropractic, as well as a Metaphysical Healer with nine books under her belt, my life's work revolves around assisting people in understanding the relevance of the unique experiences they have in life and the equal importance of the integration and attention given to the physical, emotional and spiritual aspects of the challenges we all face as human beings. Val shared how both Eastern and Western philosophies of physical and mental health play a major role in the work she does with her clients.

"It's never just about the voice".

To someone who works and writes about how an individual's biography directly impacts their biology, she was literally *singing my song.* I was wildly impressed with her extensive knowledge and experience with a variety of vocal and personal challenges, ranging from simple strain due to inappropriate use of the voice, nodules, cysts and cancer, addictions, depression and even near-death experiences. I couldn't wait to read what she had written so far.

As a Chief Editor and Head of Diversity, Inclusion and Equality at Book Hub Publishing in Ireland, I was immediately struck by the broad spectrum of stories which would appeal to audiences far greater than the niche of those interested in vocal training. Her work addresses subject matter that is of interest to everyone in the rapidly evolving world we find ourselves in today. From dealing with issues faced by transgender artists, 'one-hit wonders', to immensely talented performers who couldn't get a break due to low numbers on social media, Val covers everything from burned-out artists, the shift from physical album sales to streaming across an infinite sea of new platforms, the small-gig solo artists to the financial, relationship and health concerns faced by some of the most renowned acts around the globe.

Val takes us side-stage at major music awards, into the green rooms at televised performances, into the darkest fears of the *come-back kids*, reminding us that even the most well-known and successful artists are just people like you and me, trying to share their gifts by doing what they love. Working on this project has not only been an honor, but it has given me great faith that behind some of the most powerful and influential voices in the industry, is a deeply compassionate, fiercely dedicated professional who is directly affecting listeners by creating well-educated, conscientious and confident performers who truly want to make a difference in people's lives.

We are all simply individual expressions of frequency on the same beam of light. Val's commitment to both the physical and mental health and well-being of her students is having a profound affect, not only in the music industry, but on Broadway, the West End, Hollywood and maybe most importantly, to the aspiring singers, actors and public speakers practicing with a hairbrush in front of a mirror, in the privacy of their own homes. This book belongs in the hands of every student and teacher of performing arts. It's about time that someone shares with love, discipline and transparency, how to take personal responsibility in avoiding the pitfalls and damaging behaviors that stand between an artist and lasting success.

With absolute gratitude, love and the utmost respect for the years of study, work and dedication put in by Valerie Morehouse, I am delighted to present to you, "A Better Voice".

Dr. Mary Helen Hensley

Athlone, Ireland

INTRODUCTION

From over two decades of coaching singers, I have witnessed the power of a song. At its best, music elevates the listener and the artist above the mess of daily life, connecting us through our common life experiences. A song has the power to lift us from despair, or show us the darkest corners of our emotions. Music opens hearts and minds, reminding us of our humanity, as well as our personal truths. There is nothing in the world more powerful than frequency, and each voice carries its own unique signature. It is the privilege and task of the singer to dig deep, find their authentic voice, then share it with the world, or simply enjoy its gifts behind closed doors, if only for personal pleasure.

Finding your voice, however, does not come easy. You must do the work in order to create the feeling of effortlessness in your singing. A lot of singers skip, or minimize this essential step, because it's not as much fun as writing a song or being in the recording studio. It is the commitment to vocal technique and training that gives you the stamina for a long career, allowing you to explore your range and then share your songs as you write and sing them.

What if hitting those *difficult* high notes could be made easy? What if you could experience vocal health no matter the rigors of a demanding schedule? What if you were no longer limited by your

our own song-writing? Sounds like a dream, right? Well, it's a dream that can be turned into reality, and your journey begins by standing on the shoulders of some of the giants of the music industry, who faced the very same vocal challenges as you.

I believe everyone's voice is unique and needs personalized exercises and guidance. However, after over two decades of vocal coaching, I feel it is my responsibility to share my knowledge beyond the walls of my studio. Rather than overwhelming you with chapters full of the exercises I use with my clients, I have decided to first share some of their stories, in addition to my own experiences throughout my career to date, taking you behind the scenes and on to the front lines, giving you first-hand accounts of what it's like to be a singer in today's global entertainment industry.

At the end of the book, you will be directed to a link which will connect you to a series of master classes I have recorded with Skillshare. These tutorials will teach you how to start extending your vocal range, control your volume, and develop the skills to move smoothly from one Chamber of your voice to the next. In addition, you will be directed to the Better Voice Vocal Trainer website, a new product I am excited to endorse; one that has simplified a tried and true method of vocal training with a patented and affordable new twist on the classic straw exercises used by vocal coaches and artists around the world.

The tools found in my Skillshare master classes, as well as the Better Voice Vocal Trainer, will show you how freeing singing can and should be if you are willing to do the work. These tips and tools will first ask you to focus on how you are singing, and then, when you are ready, to let go and trust that the work you have done has been ingrained into your muscle memory so that you can focus on being an artist on the stage and in the studio.

Every day, I work with artists who sing on sold-out tours and have platinum records. Each of them has had various struggles they have worked hard to overcome through working with me in studio. I share their stories to show the work and determination it takes to make it in the music industry. I have changed names and some personal details to ensure anonymity, but their journeys and time spent in my studio, are all very real.

My methods are for singers of all levels. Whether you sing for an audience of one, or for millions, the tools and techniques I have developed over the past two decades in the trenches with my clients, can help you achieve your vocal goals, and possibly even surpass them. Music is the common language that unites us across cultures, borders, and generations. Let's dig in, find out how to do the work, unlock your potential, and take the first steps to discovering your true voice, so you may safely, comfortably and effectively use it to reach the world.

WHY I BECAME A VOCAL COACH

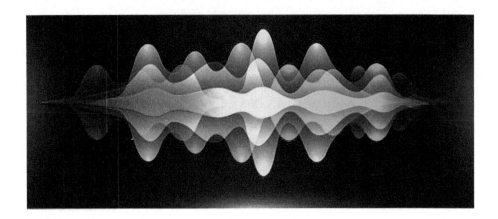

When I started writing this book, I wrestled with the question of whether or not to share my story. Would it be interesting or even relevant? But then a dear friend of mine set me straight. My vocal techniques are born out of my own journey of vocal recovery—searching, questioning, failing, and then figuring out how to right things myself. All of those small steps, and a few great leaps, are the reason I am able to empathize with the struggles, fears, and hurdles faced by my clients. I have lived everything that I teach. I have tried and tested each method on myself, often under tremendous stress and without any formal guidance. Collecting the wisdom of others, while fusing it with my own experiences, has enabled me to create a unique method. I've made it my life's work to share these tools and techniques with as many people as I can reach. This is my story.

I found happiness at the age of eight one afternoon, in the solitude of my little bedroom at 42 Honeypots Road, Surrey, England. I ran home from school that day, scampered up the stairs, and put my brand new 45 RPM vinyl of Elton John's, "Rocket Man", onto the little plastic record player my dad had given me a few days before. The song began, and I just listened. Then I joined in with Elton. Softly at first, then with more intensity. By the time I got through the first verse, I was on my own timeless flight, my rocket ship built of Bernie Taupin's lyrics, fueled, then launched by the voice and melody that is quintessential Elton John.

I let the song flow into me and out again, like clear, cool water from a mountain spring. And I sang. I really sang. My voice sounded full and mature, taking me out of the four walls of my bedroom and turning my world a clear, beautiful purple. I felt my truth. In that moment, I had a vision of the me I would become. The me I hadn't yet met. Even though my mind knew I was on my bed, in my room, my mother downstairs in the kitchen preparing dinner, in my heart, I was in another place. As I sang, I instinctively knew why I had been put here on Earth. I was here to sing. It was my calling. I knew my voice would lead others to the place Elton had led me. My fate was sealed.

That afternoon is as clear as if it were yesterday, and I relive it often. It is that same afternoon every time I hear a song simply and beautifully sung. It is that same afternoon when clients sing a clear and perfect note they couldn't reach before, because they overcame the obstacles limiting their voices. It is that same afternoon when a struggling singer does a happy dance because I've helped them to open up for the first time, so their music flows out of them, without tension, fear, or frustration. And it is that same afternoon when clients leave my studio, believing in themselves again, with growing confidence that they can sing whatever they want to, without hurting themselves.

But my story is a cautionary one. It was not very long before disaster hit. After that day on Honeypots Road, I kept singing. I sang in my bedroom, the living room, on the sidewalk walking home from school. I sang alone, I sang for my mom and dad, I sang for my friends in school. As I grew up, I joined the school choir, started a garage band, and sang in musicals. By the time I was ready to start high school, my parents had moved my brother and me to Southern California. I auditioned for my new school's elite choir, and despite the fact that I was at least three years younger than the rest of the singers, I got in. I was a lonely freshman in a sea of seniors, but I didn't care. I was singing, and I was on the fast track.

Sometime around my junior year in high school, my voice became tired. It hurt to sing. It hurt to talk. I felt like my life was collapsing around me. Singing *was* my life. It was my identity, and it was slipping away. My mom took me to see a doctor who advised I dial back my extracurriculars. So, I quit the cheerleading squad. Cheering was one of the many activities I'd thrown myself into wholeheartedly. Stopping the screaming and shouting of my cheer routines helped my voice recover enough to allow me to keep singing...so I did. I won national awards for my vocals and continued to win lead roles in every school musical. In my senior year of high school, my reputation as a vocal powerhouse was cemented. I was approached by a couple of professional musicians in their twenties who asked me to front their rock band. I didn't hesitate. Even though I was underage at eighteen years old, I sang in nightclubs all over Southern California. We did vocally challenging covers from artists such as Tower of Power, Eurythmics, Whitney Houston and more, and we did them really well.

I felt unstoppable.

One night, at a bar in Marina del Rey, a man in a purple and gold disco jacket introduced himself to me after our set. He worked in A&R for Warner Music, developing new artists. He thought I was good, and he wanted to discuss a deal. I was thrilled...ready to meet my destiny. Unfortunately, for the second time in my young life, my voice was shot. I could barely talk for days after that gig. My deal never materialized. Devastated and desperate, I went back to the doctor. After a thorough exam, he told me I had nodules on my vocal cords and gave me two options. The first was vocal rest—don't talk, don't sing, for two months. The second? Move to a humid climate. I didn't follow his advice. Instead, I bought a humidifier and rested until I thought I could dive back in. No one was going to tell me to stop singing.

I went to Chapman University on a vocal scholarship, where I majored in, then graduated with, a Bachelor of Fine Arts in Broadcast

Journalism. I sang in clubs with my dance band. I toured with the Chapman Chamber Singers, won national awards, and even studied opera. But my voice couldn't handle it. My nodules worsened, and my voice got weaker by the day. I could barely sing a lullaby. The vocal techniques I was learning at school were clearly not helping, but I couldn't stand the idea of vocal rest. So, I went to the university library (this was years before Google existed!) and searched out books about vocal anatomy and speech pathology, in an effort to find a way out of this very real dilemma. After many frustrating weeks and several dead ends, I remembered the advice of my doctor, who had suggested that a humid climate might help me to heal. As it turned out, I was dating a fellow student who was from Japan, and he had mentioned several times how humid it was there. He invited me to travel with him that summer, so I packed my bags with a few clothes and a lot of academic texts on vocal health and alternative singing techniques, hopped on a plane, and flew to Tokyo.

The humid climate, combined with the unplanned vocal rest imposed by my inability to speak the language, in addition to my trial and error efforts to strengthen my vocal cords through targeted exercises, healed my voice and eliminated my nodules. From my own successful recovery, I began to realize that there was such a thing as vocal health and healing, which started to inspire me. For the first time since Honeypots Road, I wondered if maybe there was another path for me. I began to question my dream of becoming a pop star.

When I came home to Southern California, I got a job in the marketing department of a small record distribution company. I

learned a lot about the music industry, but quickly outgr
level position, so I made the leap over to Guy Oseary an
label, Maverick Records. Watching Alanis Morissette, Ihe Prodigy,
Michelle Branch, Deftones, and many more big stars, I saw first-hand
what it took to be a professional singer. I paid attention, running
myself ragged, absorbing and learning everything I could. A stint at
Left Bank Management followed, where I was exposed to even more
artists, from Mötley Crüe, Duran Duran and John Mellencamp, to the
Bee Gees and Shania Twain. It was eye-opening, exhausting,
glamorous and intoxicating, but every day I wondered if I was in the
right place, if I was doing the right thing with my life? I knew I had
more to offer, and that my journey as a singer, who had walked
herself back from the edge of collapse, was not just a moment, but
more like... *a calling.*

After seven years on the business side of the music industry, the
little voice inside me that constantly questioned my career choices
got a lot louder. I was at an impasse. So, I went home and sought the
advice of my father, who, at the time, was fighting a losing battle with
cancer. He told me seven words I have never forgotten.

"Valerie, leap and the net will appear."

Only a few weeks later, we lost him. But through his words, I had
found the courage to pursue a new path. I quit my comfortable job
and set out to start a business of my own. I would be on the frontlines
with singers, helping them to overcome injuries, and grow into their
true selves. I stretched the bounds of vocal coaching by immersing
myself in the study of vocal anatomy and pathology. I convinced

doctors who specialized in the voice to let me watch them work, and I asked questions…so many questions. As I gathered priceless knowledge about vocal health, I also realized there was a need for vocal coaches who could help rehabilitate singers after injury and surgery. That was it—my niche. I was on my way.

Today, I still sing all the time. I love it. But what I love even more, is the opportunity to help facilitate the discovery process and subsequent healing journey with each of my clients. When I can look at terrified or despairing new clients and tell them with absolute confidence and certainty that they can overcome their struggles and succeed, there is no better feeling than watching the fear leave their eyes. I work with artists who think their careers are ending because they have lost control of their unique sounds. I am so fortunate that I get to guide them through the empowering process of recovery. Some of my clients have platinum records, yet come to me because they cannot sing live. Seeing their dedication to the tools I give them and watching them successfully tour the world is incredibly motivating as a coach. Nearly every day I witness miraculous transformations and my current career, my public and private life, are more fulfilling than I could have ever dreamed.

Now, I will take you behind the scenes to the music industry's front lines. It is my honor to share some of my clients' incredible stories, while explaining how I have realized a personal vision, by creating practical tools which allow me to guide some of the world's greatest voices to their highest potential. But first, a simple anatomy lesson and an inside view of what every client who crosses my threshold must learn, before we ever sing a single note.

HOW DOES YOUR VOICE WORK?

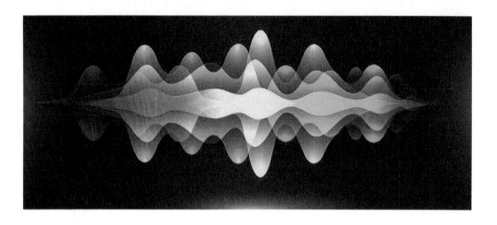

"I had certain goals and aspirations as a singer that I couldn't get to without Valerie. She showed me the way to make singing much easier and fun. Now I love singing."

—Deryck Whibley, *SUM 41*, Lead Singer

What if I told you I was going to give you a sports car. Let's say a Ferrari or a Lamborghini. Pretty cool, right? I'll just hand you the keys, tuck you into the driver's seat, set you loose on an open racetrack, and send you on your way. Zero to a hundred in six seconds. Keep in mind, it's a stick shift. Never driven one? How about that tricky steering wheel? Rounding a sharp bend at top speed? Careful, or you'll overturn and spin out.

The voice is like a super-powered, highly sensitive sports car—most of us can figure out how to turn it on, but do not know how to use the fiddly gear shift, let alone how to get the best performance out of this top-of-the-line piece of machinery. Back before I learned about my voice, I assumed, like many singers, that just because I could speak, I automatically knew how to sing. What I didn't realize, is that my voice is a complex instrument in need of the same attention as if I was learning the guitar, piano or drums. How about I offer you a quick overview about how your own voice works, so you can learn to whip around those turns at 190mph. There's nothing quite like the freedom of singing with a fully engaged voice. Let's get to know one of the most fascinating instruments in your vehicle; your voice.

STEP INTO MY STUDIO

Every singer who steps into my studio for the first time receives a warm welcome and then, an unexpected pop quiz. As I take them through a series of diagnostic exercises, I ask them four questions:

1. What are your vocal cords made of?
2. What is your larynx and what is its function?
3. What are the three Chambers of your voice?
4. Where are those Chambers supposed to resonate?

Most of my singers do not know the answers, so as we go through the session, I show them where each part of their voice is located and what it does. Of course, a lot of people can sing and some even sell millions of records without knowing the first thing about their voice, or how it works. It is true that you do not need to know the ins and outs of the voice in order to sing. But if you want to get the most out of your instrument, reach your vocal potential, and stay healthy over time, then understanding your anatomy *is a must*. I haven't had a single singer at my studio who didn't want to find out how they could be better, while learning how to safe-guard their voice against vocal injuries.

THE SPA

I'm not talking about a day spa! All the parts of your body that work together to create sound, I call the **SPA**—your **Sound Producing Anatomy**:

A. Three Chambers of the Voice: Chest, Mix, and Head.

B. Vocal Cords.

C. Larynx

D. Sinus cavities, nose, nasal cavities, mouth, tongue, lips, teeth, hard palate, soft palate, esophagus, windpipe, lungs, diaphragm, rib cage, and sternum.

HOW DOES YOUR VOICE WORK?

- The lowest register of the voice
- Deeper, thicker tonality
- Feel vibrations in your chest
- The vocal register you speak in

- Has power and intensity
- Can go high without tension or strain

- Feel vibration sensations in your head
- Has a more gentle tonality with less power than chest voice

To start, we will focus on A, B, and C. The **Three Chambers of the voice** should work together as one seamless sound, from the **Chest Voice** resonating in the chest, the **Mix Voice** resonating primarily in the nose and mouth, to the **Head Voice** resonating in the forehead and in the back and top of the head. The **vocal cords** are two bands of muscle and tissue, which is why, through focused exercises, they can be strengthened. If they are not used properly, over time, they can be damaged. Vocal cords are located inside the **larynx (or voice box)**, which is also made of muscle, acting like a valve to help regulate airflow while singing.

Did you notice the only muscles I mentioned in the neck that are part of the SPA are the vocal cords and larynx? What about all those singers with veins popping out of their neck when screaming the high notes? It is all unnecessary, and worse, damaging. If you are singing this way, then you are causing undue stress and harm to your SPA. I have seen it time and time again. Those singers will often wind up in my studio, dealing with loss of vocal range, cancelled shows, frantically seeking answers.

***

A boy's changing voice during puberty can be a scary time. This can be even more unsettling when he is a singer. I have had a number of male clients who, before their voice changed, sang for kids' cartoon series, in award-winning children's choirs, or already had a successful career with chart-topping singles. Going into the unknown of what pitch his singing voice is finally going to settle in, can be incredibly unnerving. Each teenage boy's experience is different, and it is important to have a vocal coach who understands the SPA, to gradually adjust vocal exercises and range to help smooth out the transition as much as possible.

I have several transgender clients whose voices have transitioned or are in the process of transitioning. The focus is always on adjusting the range of the exercises towards the range of the gender they identify with. Working on finding their true voice and expansion of range is such an exhilarating and special time for them, and I love coaching them through this voyage. It is incredible what the human voice can achieve when free of self and societal imposed limitations.

Working with LGBTQ+ clients, I realized there are hundreds of books out there about the voice and singing, however, they all refer to the *male* and *female* voices. As a vocal coach, these are familiar terms, however, these antiquated ideas can limit the true potential of an artist's voice. I have male clients who are well able to sing up into the traditionally *female* ranges, and female clients who have an incredibly rich, lower *male* range. One of the things that is important to me in this book is for everyone who reads it to feel included; unlimited by gender. Expanding your range above or below the 'norms' associated with your physicality, is not a competition, but rather an organic and fluid process which will occur naturally as you strengthen your SPA.

YOUR UNIQUE SOUND

So what makes your voice *yours*? To project sound, we use the **Three Chambers** of the voice—Chest, Mix, and Head. Let us go ahead and fill in the picture a little further. Each of the chambers provides a home for the different sound frequencies, or notes, that make up the musical scale. (The throat and neck are not included in the three chambers of the voice, because your sound should not be focused to this area. It is not an effective resonance chamber. If you place your sound in your throat and neck, the muscles will tense and this will lead to a misalignment of the vocal cords, which can lead to vocal damage). As the sound exits the body through your larynx and vocal cords, it is shaped by the soft palate and hard palate on the roof of the mouth, tongue, teeth, and lips. These, combined with the three chambers of your voice, give you your unique sound.

VOCAL CORDS

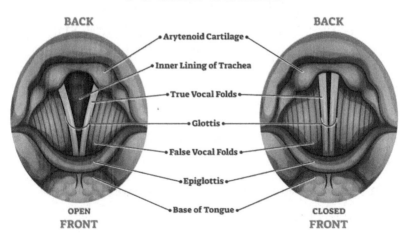

BACK — Arytenoid Cartilage — BACK

Inner Lining of Trachea

True Vocal Folds

Glottis

False Vocal Folds

Epiglottis

OPEN — Base of Tongue — CLOSED
FRONT — FRONT

YOUR TRUE VOICE

Although your distinct sound is created by your SPA, it is affected by the combination of your personality, identity, intellect, and emotions, when you speak or sing. You should strive to produce the purest, most honest version of your voice. The voice that is unique only to you. I call that your *true voice*. Your true voice does not require you to think about how you want to sound, but rather is the result of just letting go, allowing yourself to experience the sound that comes naturally when you relax and release your SPA. Nurturing your true voice is the foundation of a great voice. It is the voice your body was meant to create, and it is created only with a free and open SPA.

This is why it is so important to take the time to understand all the parts of the SPA and integrate them. Once you have mastered them, you can let go and allow your true voice to work in the widest range of tones which gives your voice its unique qualities. Having multiple tones to draw from is essential as a singer, because tones are what color the voice. If you only sing with one tone, it is like listening to someone speaking in a monotone voice. Poor integration of the SPA limits tonal quality. Imagine you live in a five thousand square foot home, and you spend all of your time in the kitchen. Thousands of beautiful square feet would go unused. The same principle applies if you try to sing all of your songs in chest voice and do not engage your mix voice to get into your head voice. It is wasted potential. The SPA should be like a house with an open floor plan— you can easily move from room to room, with no breaks or obstacles.

Singers should be able to hear *and* feel the notes they sing. To become a good singer you must become aware of what happens when you sing. By getting to know your voice through understanding how your SPA works, you will get to know your limitations so that you can learn to strengthen your SPA to overcome them. Do you flinch at hitting high notes? Do you sing too loudly? Too softly? Do you struggle to articulate? Do you know how to adjust your vowels to make certain words easier to sing?

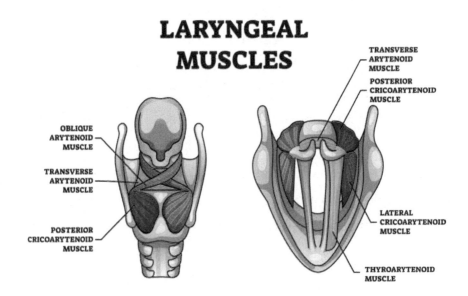

LARYNGEAL MUSCLES

OBLIQUE ARYTENOID MUSCLE

TRANSVERSE ARYTENOID MUSCLE

POSTERIOR CRICOARYTENOID MUSCLE

TRANSVERSE ARYTENOID MUSCLE

POSTERIOR CRICOARYTENOID MUSCLE

LATERAL CRICOARYTENOID MUSCLE

THYROARYTENOID MUSCLE

BEHIND THE SCENES: DISCOVERING THE MIX

🎼 came to me at the height of a career that had already spanned two decades. Over the course of those years, she had become one of the world's most recognizable and successful pop singers. There was no one like her. Her boundary-pushing artistry captivated sold-out stadiums. But she had a problem. She was struggling to sing her own songs. She was preparing to leave on a world tour when she contacted me, humbled and frustrated. We emailed and spoke a few times before agreeing to meet at my studio. She dodged the paparazzi and her ever-present entourage, and drove herself to our first session. I quickly got to work assessing her voice.

🎼 has a voice that is tonally rich—her natural gifts were clear. She is one of the most powerful singers to ever set foot in my studio. But just as clear as her many gifts, was her habit of aggressively forcing her voice into the higher registers, where most of her songs were written. To a fan watching her show, her vein-popping sound might have seemed like a passionate performance, but in reality, it was a destructive one.

I took 🎼 through my vocal diagnostic, where it was immediately apparent that she wasn't connecting to her Mix voice. She had a powerful and natural Chest voice, as well as an operatic Head voice she had learned from one of her teachers along the way. What she didn't know, was how to shift into that all important middle gear. As a result, she was pulling her Chest voice up way too high, which choked her out, subsequently causing damage. This was an unsustainable approach. I knew she would never last on tour unless we made some very important changes to engage her Mix voice.

A note about the Mix voice. It is called the Mix voice because it uses two resonance Chambers. When you are singing in chest voice and start to go a little higher in your range, your Chest voice should start to blend with your Mix voice seamlessly. As you sing higher notes, your Chest voice should become less engaged, as your Mix voice should start to blend into your Head voice. The same happens in reverse as you go back down to your lower range. Just as an athlete works the abdomen and lower back to strengthen the core, the Mix voice is essentially the core of your voice, which makes it one of the most important tools in a singer's toolkit. There are some prominent vocal coaches who believe that there is only Chest and Head voice, or if they do know about the Mix voice, they do not use the most effective approaches to strengthen it. I have encountered many of these students, who find their way to me after years of vocal strain and discouragement, from trying to unsuccessfully extend and create smooth transitions through their range.

Before I had 𝄞 sing another note, I took her through my four SPA questions to get a baseline on her level of knowledge about her voice. Unsurprisingly, like most of my clients, she didn't know the basics. She was speeding around the racetrack, grinding the gears, and oversteering her Ferrari, which would have eventually led to a complete and total breakdown.

I walked her through a series of exercises to help her feel her SPA at work. As she sang through each one, she told me she started feeling things with her voice she had never felt before. These exercises, although simple, have a profound impact, especially for someone like 𝄞, who had spent the better part of her life as a professional singer. After so many years on the stage, it is easy for a singer to think there is nothing more to know, nothing new to learn. Before we finished our session together, she stopped and said, "I now realize I haven't been using my voice to its full potential."

By the time her tour started, 𝄞 was singing through her set list with ease and confidence. Taking the time to learn how her voice worked and how to take care of her instrument, she was armed with the tools she needed to stay at the top of her game during her tour. Her powerful performances became even more passionate and captivating. As I waited in the wings at the Hollywood Bowl before the start of her show, her manager, an industry veteran who had nurtured his fair share of artists, approached me and said, "I've worked with her for thirteen years and she's never sounded this good." There is always room for improvement in your vocals, no matter what stage you are at, or on, in your career.

DO YOU NEED TO WARM UP?

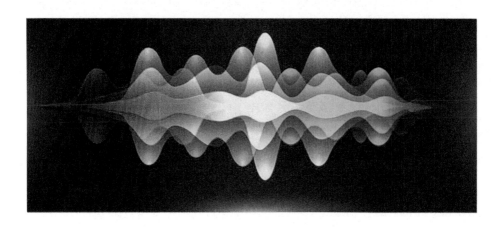

"When I met Valerie, I didn't have a voice outside the studio. Over a year of consistent vocal training with Val, I am now singing confidently at over one hundred and fifty shows a year."

—Drew Taggart, *The Chainsmokers*, Lead Singer

Oscar Hammerstein got it right when he wrote the lyrics to the *Sound of Music's* legendary song, "Do Re Mi". In the movie, Julie Andrews' iconic soprano voice teaches, "When you read you begin with ABC. When you sing you begin with Do Re Mi." It's *almost* that simple. The beginning *is* always Do Re Mi. The scale. It is the foundation upon which all songs are built. It is also the classic singer's warm-up; the simplest and perhaps least valued or used tool

in most singer's toolkits. Like Oscar and Julie, I will keep
you don't warm up, you won't sing to your full potential. Perio..

If you have hopes of a successful singing career or a goal such as singing at your friend's wedding or even winning a karaoke competition, then you must warm up your voice properly. Why? In the last chapter, I mentioned your vocal cords are made of muscle. Like all muscles in the body, the voice must be carefully stretched before expecting it to operate at its best, not to mention to avoid the risk of injury. This cannot be overstated. *A singer is an athlete*, and just like all athletes, proper training and preparation are necessary for success, no matter what the goal. If every singer committed to doing a few targeted vocal warm-ups every day, we would see a huge reduction in the number of vocal injuries, with an increase in the consistency and quality of performances. So why don't singers warm up? Because warm-ups aren't always fun. We want to jump in and sing our songs; just like at the gym when we want to immediately start running a mile instead of getting a mat out to stretch our muscles first. In addition, many singers do not have the right vocal warm-ups for their voice, so they cannot experience the benefit, or even worse, their voice might hurt after attempting to warm up.

BEHIND THE SCENES: BACK TO THE BEGINNING

🎵 was one of my most promising students. She was a young and gifted singer from a family of Grammy award-winning artists. We first met in her private recording studio. Her manager, a long-time friend of mine, greeted me at the door. I went in, as I always do, with no expectations. I knew she wanted to achieve the musical success enjoyed by the other members of her family, and that she had a recording contract with a major label, with a team of industry professionals banking on her success. I was brought in to ensure that she could give it her best shot.

They invited me to sit on a deep, leather couch, from which I could see her family's gold and platinum records lining the walls. 🎶 took her place at the keyboard, and I could see she was nervous. She pushed through and sang one of her original, unpublished songs. It was good. *She was good.* Her voice was warm and rich and had a soulfulness beyond her years. I could see why the record label was excited about her. She finished her song, and then sang another, and another. Then it was my turn.

The first thing I ask of any client is that they sing a scale. Up to the top of their vocal range and back down again. Back to the beginning—Do Re Mi. The scale lays the voice bare.

You can't fake your way through it. No impressive vocal riffs or scooping into the pitch. It's one of the hardest things I ever ask my clients to do. As I listen to one note after another, I can identify where the singer struggles, where their voice breaks, and where it becomes breathy, unsupported or strained. I take about five minutes to initially diagnose a singer's vocal personality, and then I begin to give them the tools to strengthen their voice.

♫ approached the scales with a combination of fear and uncertainty. She, like most singers, wanted me to immediately start working through her songs. The scales, by comparison, were not very exciting. But she trusted her manager, who referred her to me, and went through my process. Her voice, though rich, lacked strength in the upper registers. It became forced and strained at the B flat above Middle C—a female voice's first break. She was using her neck muscles to heave herself over the break... a common, but potentially very damaging approach. Once, on the other side of her break, the notes became breathy and weak, because her voice lacked strength and mobility as it transitioned. She had a good ear, but these vocal weaknesses caused her to become pitchy in her Mix and Head voice.

In spite of this issue, I heard the potential, and I told her I thought she could out sing any member of her family, *if she was willing to do the work.* I meant every word. I could tell she wanted to believe me, but at the time, it sounded like a fairy-tale to her. We agreed to meet once a week in the months leading up to her first scheduled tour dates. She was nervous, carrying the weight of the expectations from her family's achievements, as well as those of the record label, on her young shoulders. I assured her we would overcome her limitations and give her the tools to achieve her goals and dreams.

BEGIN

The exercise programs I create for my clients in my studio are personalized to address their specific vocal challenges, there are a series of basic warm-ups I recommend for all my singers. But first, you must identify your primary vocal personality. We all have one. What we do not all have, are the *right tools* to know how to recognize which personality your voice has. This is where I come in.

Just like we have different personalities in life, we also have different vocal personalities.

There are two main categories, **Type A** *and* **Type B**. *Some people use too much muscle to push through the breaks in their voices; those are Type A. Others disengage as they go through their breaks and use too much air, which creates a breathy sound; those are Type B. Most singers fall into one of these two categories. A singer sometimes has a bit of both, but typically everyone has a primary vocal personality. Even advanced, well-trained singers still have a primary, base-line vocal personality. It is much harder to detect because they have trained their voices to transition smoothly, but when they are tired or sick, they will have a tendency to revert to their vocal personality, Type A (strain) or Type B (breathy). This is why it is so important to discover which vocal personality you have and use the tools that help to balance your voice and SPA.*

When ♫ arrived at my studio a week after our first meeting, she was excited to get to work, but also unsure of herself and her chances of success. We sang up and down the Five Tone Ah scale, and she struggled in the same way and in the same places as before, but this time, the challenges at her vocal break were even more acute. **Type A, all the way!** I knew exactly what was causing the problem. *She was terrified.* Her fears were compounding her vocal weaknesses. I'll be the first to admit that I have a strong personality, but I am not scary. I knew her fears had very little to do with me or my studio, and everything to do with her self-esteem and the pressure from her managers, the record label, and her family. You cannot sing well if you are afraid.

Scales can boost your confidence as you start to build your singer's toolkit, but they will not quiet your inner critic or chase away your deepest fears. If every time you open your mouth to sing, you are confronted by feelings of inadequacy, or a memory of the time you were passed up for a role in your school musical, you are always going to be held back. Maybe a lot, maybe just a little, but until you acknowledge and do the work necessary to minimize, or better still, defeat your inner demons, they will always be there, sabotaging your singing.

So I gave 🎵 a non-musical exercise. I asked her to write down on a piece of paper all the scary things she felt when she sang. Fear of failure, fear of success, feelings of inadequacy, fear of forgetting the lyrics, whatever it was for her. After she finished, I told her to rip it up into tiny pieces and throw them away. This may seem like a crazy thing to do, but it is a powerful exercise. First, recognizing and writing down the fears and expectations holding you back diminishes their power over you. Second, by ripping up the paper, you symbolically destroy your fears, as a first step toward creating a new, more positive script for your life. We will explore more strategies to conquer your fears in the Skillshare master classes links at the end of the book.

🎵 had effectively overcome her Type A tendency at her first vocal break, after only two weeks, a few sessions with me, and fifteen minutes a day of targeted arpeggios at home. She was thrilled with her new found ability to sing smoothly through her Mix and Head voice and was expanding her range. We continued to work together for several more months before agreeing that she was ready to get on the stage. We saw each other less often and only via Skype. She traveled with her managers through Europe, singing and building a fan base. Things were going really well. But as is often the case, she started down a slippery slope that so many performers gravitate towards, when they think their problems have simply disappeared. 🎵 had stopped doing her warm-ups consistently. That's when I got the call.

Her musical director was in a mild panic. 🎵 was scheduled to perform on a major late-night talk show, a huge opportunity, and her vocals had taken a serious downturn. I agreed to meet them at the television lot to assess the situation and see what we could do to prop her up in the few short hours before she was scheduled to be taped for the show. When I arrived at the studio, I first saw her mother. She told me that her daughter sounded pitchy, then added, "When she was with you, she was perfect." I thought to myself, *When she was with me, she was consistently working on her vocal exercises.*

DO YOU NEED TO WARM UP?

Sure enough, when I took 🎵 through her exercises, she admitted that she had not done these exercises for weeks. She didn't have to tell me as her voice gave everything away. Her old tendency towards Type A had resurfaced, and she had lost power in her Mix and Head voice. But all our work together had built a foundation of muscle memory that helped her recover some ground quickly before her big moment on television. The performance went well. Everyone breathed a sigh of relief, and she promised never to compromise on her vocal exercises again.

🎵 continued to do the morning and late-night talk show circuit, both at home and abroad. Another few months went by before I saw her again, this time, backstage at the iHeart Radio Music Awards to warm her up. She promised me she had been diligent about her vocal exercises. When she sang for me during her warm-up, her voice corroborated her story. She sounded amazing. At that moment, I knew she was ready to go to the next level. She had the tools she needed to succeed, as well as the discipline to use them.

This story is not unique. I have seen it play out dozens of times. Promising clients who come to me with natural talent, work hard for a few months, think they have trained enough, and off they go. Done and done. But expecting your voice to stay in shape after a short series of sessions is like going to the gym just long enough to meet your goals and then relaxing on your laurels *and the couch,* eating pizza. How long do you think your abs will stay ripped?

Any athlete knows it would be crazy to think they could succeed without training. Serena Williams is a perfect example. She is one of the greatest tennis players of all time, but she has said she doesn't enjoy training. However, in order to stay at the top of her game, she knows she has to commit to her workout routine. Does she have a natural talent for the sport? Absolutely. But a lot of people have natural talent. It is what Serena does with her natural talent that makes the difference. Let us be clear. Singing well, especially at the professional level, is an athletic pursuit. As a vocal coach, all I am asking is that you commit to fifteen short minutes a day, training your voice by doing the exercises designed for your vocal tendencies, in order to strengthen your muscles. It's a small sacrifice, that over time, will make your vocals bionic.

VOCAL CHECK-UP TIME

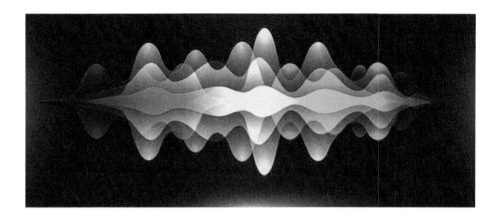

"When I lost my voice and had to get vocal cord surgery to recover, Val was there to help. An incredible voice coach. I'm happy that she was there when I needed her!"

—Steve Aoki, DJ/Producer

In today's music industry, being a pop star is every bit the athletic undertaking as that of someone training for the Olympics. Gold medallist, Usain Bolt, said, "Skill is only developed by hours and hours of hard work." This may sound extreme, but behind the scenes, the life of a pop star is not all parties and island vacations.

Back in the day, singers got most of their income from selling records, cassette tapes, and CDs, but now that streaming services have taken over, a major shift has occurred. Tour tickets and merchandise sales have taken over as the money-makers. This means that labels and managers are booking more and more tour dates and gigs. On average, a professional singer will travel and perform at least forty to sixty major tour shows a year, as well as singing at over one hundred smaller venues, high profile award shows, in addition to countless radio shows and promotional events. To prep for tour, they will rehearse eight hours or more a day for a set that lasts at least one hour and if they are the headliner, often two hours. During these sets, most singers also dance, run, jump, or even do cirque du sol-esque acts on top of singing... *without a break*. This is not something a singer can keep up with on a back-to-back tour schedule, without a high level of physical fitness. But even more important than the large muscle groups that sustain a singer's energy, are the much smaller muscles that are used when we sing. The muscles in the SPA (Sound Producing Anatomy) are the muscles that the singer works the hardest. Vocal injuries occur for many of the same reasons as those faced by other athletes: not warming up properly, lack of stamina, not taking the time to vocal rest, and traumatic incidents. To stay at the top of your game as a singer, you must not only understand how your voice works, but you must consistently work on and adapt your technique. This includes understanding the limits of your voice, accepting the need to take time to rest and recover after practicing and performing.

The information I am sharing is to show you the importance of looking after your voice. If you are dealing with a vocal issue or injury, this information will give you a basic overview to help you better understand what is happening, while you work with your voice doctor, aka **Laryngologist**. I am not a medical doctor and cannot medically diagnose your vocals. If you think you have any issue with your SPA, especially your vocal cords, make an appointment with a voice doctor who has a record of working with singers. Do not try to self-diagnose or fix it without a medical professional's guidance.

VOCAL INJURIES

The most common and often devastating vocal cord injuries suffered by people who overuse or improperly use their voices are:

1. Nodules—soft and hard
2. Cysts
3. Polyps
4. Scarring
5. Hemorrhages
6. Vocal Dysphonia

Whether we sing for a living or for fun, bad habits and poor technique leave our delicate vocal cords vulnerable to damage. Some of these injuries can cause permanent harm to your voice, and the rise in vocal injuries for singers is happening at near epidemic levels compared to ten years ago. So what's going wrong? Of course, the decline of record sales and the rise of music streaming services was a huge part of starting this spiral, as labels and managers had to find alternative revenue streams for their artists. Other factors include that the popular styles of singing today can be much harder on the voice without proper technique training. In many cases, vocal injuries are being caused by overuse. It is not just singers who are at risk, but also professional speakers, sports announcers, call center employees, and even people who just like to talk a lot. How can we fix it? In certain cases, when an injury or a genetic condition is present, surgery can be the best option. I collaborate with many Laryngologists, who are doctors that specialize in the voice. While techniques and diagnosis may differ, they all agree on one thing. **Prevention is key**. Proper training and technique are the best preventative medicines.

A well-documented example of the perils of vocal overuse is Adele, one of the world's most acclaimed and successful artists. She had to cancel her world tour not once, but twice, to have surgery to repair her vocal cords. Although a small number of Laryngologists still advise that repeated surgeries on the vocal cords are the only choice, there are far more who believe very strongly that other, less invasive steps, can and should be taken first. Before we go any further, let me be clear, there are some instances, such as in the case of a hard nodule, where surgery by a skilled physician, preceded and followed by vocal rehabilitation to heal and prevent further injury, is the best option. But in many cases, I have experienced that the injury can be healed, or even better, prevented, with a balance of vocal rest prescribed by a voice doctor and the introduction of specific vocal exercises to rehabilitate.

How do you know if you have a vocal injury? It is virtually impossible to know with one hundred percent certainty without having your throat scoped by a voice doctor. That said, there are three key indicators that should sound alarm bells. These are the same things I look for when I meet every new client.

FIRST INDICATOR

First, let's start with your speaking voice. Is your voice raspy? Do you feel like certain words catch in your throat? Do you find yourself unable to complete certain words because the sound falls off at the end? This could be a sign of overuse without damage, or you might have something on the vocal cords causing this.

SECOND INDICATOR

Are you struggling to make it through or past your first vocal break when singing a scale or on specific notes? Usually, if you are experiencing difficulty here, it is more likely that your vocal cords are healthy. However, because of a lack of technique, you may be using your neck muscles to sing, causing vocal strain to your SPA. This can be resolved with a little bit of training. It is important to be aware, that struggling to connect between notes could also indicate allergies, post-nasal drip, or acid reflux, or it could be something bigger such as nodules, cysts, or hemorrhages, not allowing your vocal cords to function optimally.

THIRD INDICATOR

Finally, try to vocalize the sound of a police siren through an open mouth (not a hum). A high toned *wooOOOooo* that goes from soft to loud, back to soft. If you have a vocal injury, this will most likely be nearly impossible to accomplish. You might find yourself beginning but not able to finish the siren, especially in the higher registers. Or you might make a sound closer to that of air escaping from a balloon. If you have a conventional male voice or you are a new, untrained singer, this exercise can be difficult because your vocal cords are not used to singing that high. Just like muscles in the body, your vocal cords will need to be trained to work at a higher performance level.

While any one of the above indicators is not enough to arrive at a diagnosis, if you are experiencing any of them, and especially if you are experiencing all three, the best course of action is to get your throat scoped by a voice doctor. Best case scenario, you waste a few hours at the doctor's office to discover there is nothing wrong with you (other than needing to strengthen your SPA to avoid injury in the future). But if you do have an issue with your vocal cords or another part of your SPA, you will be able to tackle it head on, with a clear understanding of the source of your issue.

Your doctor may suggest vocal surgery, but always ask your doctor about the possible benefits of **vocal rest**. In some cases, a voice doctor will require a patient to take a week or more of vocal rest to reduce vocal cord swelling before they can even perform a diagnostic scope.

Vocal rest is something my clients, and most professional singers and actors, are stubbornly resistant to doing. A treatment plan that includes vocal rest is asking the patient to commit to absolute silence for a prescribed period of time—no whispering, no laughing, no singing, no talking. This is a very scary thing for people who rely on their voices for their livelihoods. Just give vocal rest a try for an hour. You will be surprised how many times you need or want to make a sound. Now multiply that to three weeks along with the pressures of the professional singer or actor; the fear of losing gigs and their careers suffering; they will do anything to avoid the silence.

This is one reason why many professional singers will opt for the surgical route even if there are less invasive options. They believe that it is the quickest, most sure-fire path to recovery. *But consider this.* If your doctor is suggesting surgery, many surgeons require one week of full vocal rest for their patients before committing to surgery. Then after surgery, there are usually two more weeks of complete vocal rest for the patient. This is the same time commitment as the non-surgical route, so why not consider the long game and try the less invasive option first? It's true, you could commit yourself to three weeks of complete vocal rest only to find that you will still need surgery, but this is rare. Keep in mind, that all surgeries are not without risk.

Vocal rest is not just for vocal injuries, it is an essential part of preventing injury. My touring clients will tell you that I have recommended vocal rest for all of them at some point or another. During our FaceTime warm-ups, I may start to hear a slight weakness in an area of their voice that wasn't there before, so I will ask them to vocal rest on their next day off, as well as in between all promos and meet and greets. Short periods of vocal rest on tour can work wonders in preventing vocal weaknesses turning into an injury.

SURGERY AND REHAB

Having eliminated my own soft nodules and many of my clients' soft nodules and polyps over my twenty-five-year career, I can attest to the superpower of vocal rehabilitation through vocal rest, exercises, and technique training. Soft nodules and polyps can do very well with vocal rest and technique adjustments alone.

Now, if you have been diagnosed with a large hemorrhage, hard nodule, or cyst, all of these generally require surgical intervention. Do your homework, select a well-respected surgeon who specializes in working with singers, and find out *before* surgery what you should plan to do for vocal rehabilitation. Planning out your recovery after surgery is vital. Unless your vocal cord injury is from something you were born with, such as a congenital cyst, it is most likely that your injury was caused by lack of proper vocal technique. If you have surgery on your voice and do not change how you are singing and/or speaking, you are destined to experience the same injury again and again. As Einstein famously said,

"The definition of insanity is doing the same thing over and over again and expecting different results."

BEHIND THE SCENES: BE SAFE NOT SORRY

If available, I always prefer to use the least invasive methods available to heal my clients, but I will be the first one to send a client to a voice doctor if there is even a small chance that they have a vocal injury. I don't hesitate. As a cautionary tale, and to motivate those of you who may be resistant to visiting the doctor, I will share with you 𝄢's almost fatal mistake. 𝄢 is a very prominent motivational speaker who was introduced to me by a mutual friend. He had been having trouble with his speaking voice for months but had refused to downsize his packed schedule in order to seek help. He lived in another state, meaning we couldn't initially meet face to face, so I scheduled a phone meeting through his assistant.

From his first "Hello" on the other end of the line, I knew he had a serious problem. His speaking voice was one of the worst I had ever heard. His words would fall away, and the breathy, raspy quality of every sentence was painful to hear. He acknowledged that he had been dealing with this for a long time and that he had prioritized his career over his health—an all too common and sometimes disastrous decision. After he told me his story, I asked him to stop speaking and to listen to me very carefully. I told him that the moment we hung up the phone, he should immediately call the voice doctor I recommended, and insist on being seen the next day. I assured him that his business would survive without him for the time it would take to seek help.

Weeks went by without a word from 𝄢. I worried a lot. Then one day, a little more than a month later, my phone rang. It was him. He sounded like a new man. He told me that he had gone to see a doctor the very next day, as I recommended, where he was diagnosed with stage four throat cancer. He would have died in a few short months without surgical intervention and radiation therapy. It was a very close call, but he emerged with a determination to work hard at keeping his SPA healthy. The radiation had left his vocal cords significantly weakened, so we strategized a course of vocal rehab that included increasingly challenging vocal exercises to get him back to work as quickly and safely as possible. He is now healthy and still at the top of his game. To this day, his story stands out as one of the most profound, and touching, of my career.

***

Vocal rehabilitation that combines vocal technique training with vocal rest, is an essential part of healing the voice after an injury, whether or not surgery is required. To show how vocal rehab has a vital role during recovery, I'm going to share two stories less extreme than 𝄢's, though equally transformative.

BEHIND THE SCENES: EARTHY ISN T ALWAYS NATURAL

♭ came to me at the start of her career. She was born into Hollywood royalty. She played clubs in Hollywood and private events here and there, but I was wondering why she hadn't yet recorded any of her original works.

When she arrived in my studio for the first time, her wardrobe gave a Mother Earth or *hippie* vibe, but her energy said something else. She was nervous and unsure. When she spoke, the first thing I noticed was the unnatural tone in her voice. It sounded forced, and put on. This was my first red flag. A person who deliberately works to change the natural tone of their voice in favor of something they find more appealing, is overtaxing their vocal cords with every word they speak. After we exchanged a few pleasantries I took her through my standard diagnostic. *At least I tried.* ♭'s range was limited to five notes. They sounded evocative and sexy, but you don't have to be a vocal coach to know that you won't get far into a singing career with a range that limits you to five notes.

I had her sing the notes again and listened very carefully. It was clear to me that something was disrupting the natural action of her vocal cords, so I knew a trip to a voice doctor would be the necessary next step. No one wants to hear this, and ♭ was no exception. Still, she took my recommendation to heart, and later that week, she visited with the doctor I referred her to. Her diagnosis? She had soft nodules and scarring on her left vocal cord, which her doctor said was probably from speaking with a 'vocal fry' (dropping the voice to its lowest register until it crackles) and yelling through her shows with improper technique. The doctor and I determined that the scarring was irreversible but, given the nodules' size and placement, they could be alleviated with a combination of speech therapy and vocal rehabilitation.

♭ and I worked together for just over a month. I taught her about her SPA and walked her through the process of learning to feel the three Chambers of her voice activate as she sang. The muscles in her neck began to relax. We worked on returning her speaking voice to its natural tone, and as she became more and more skilled, we introduced vocal warm-ups of increasing complexity. About two weeks into our work together, she began to feel measurably better. So much so, that she began to accept performance opportunities without checking in with me and her doctor first. This was not a good idea. Diving into performances in the middle of rehabbing a damaged vocal cord is like taking a bicycle onto the hardest off-road trail you can find on the same day you take off the training wheels. You are setting yourself up for a fall. I had to convince ♭ to decline gigs until the doctor and I had determined that she was fully healed. It didn't take long. About six weeks after we began to work together, she had another vocal scope. The nodules were gone. This determined young lady had come out on the other side of our work with healthy vocal cords and a much better understanding of how to keep her singing and speaking voice injury free. She had also gained an additional octave in vocal range. She was off to a beautiful start to what would soon prove to be a very promising career.

In ♭'s case, we were able to avoid surgery by rehabbing her voice and ending her destructive vocal habits. For the cases where vocal surgery is recommended, it is still every bit as important to rehab the vocal cords, before and after surgery. This was the case in the next story.

BEHIND THE SCENES: FROM UNSURE TO UNLIMITED

𝄽 was a *one-hit wonder*. At least, that is how her destiny was shaping up. When she came to me her head was still spinning from the thrill of what many saw as an overnight success, but her heart was in tumult because she had a secret, she thought was too terrible to face. The song she had written, that had found its way to the top of the charts, was written around her limited vocal ability. She couldn't sing much of anything else. Record deals were being written, opportunities for live performances were being set, and she was in a panic. My studio would become her safe haven.

We began, as I always do, with the exercises that reveal everything I need to know about a singer's strengths and weaknesses, their road ahead, and the issues that brought them to me. 𝄽's voice showed all the classic signs of vocal cord damage. It was rough and scratchy, her range limited, she was experiencing tightness in her neck, and she had almost no vocal stamina. A few arpeggios and her voice tired. It was clear she had something on her vocal cords, but in order to know exactly what, we would need the intervention and expertise of a trained voice doctor.

Her doctor identified a fluid filled sac, a cyst, on one of her vocal cords. Given the number of years ⸄ said her symptoms had been present, essentially as long as she could remember, and the size and placement of the cyst, it was determined that the condition was likely congenital. It had been with her from the day she was born. The only way to access her full vocal potential was to surgically remove the cyst. The surgery was scheduled a month out, giving ⸄ and me enough time to start rehabilitating her voice, as well as establishing new and healthy singing habits before her operation. The reason it is so important to start vocal rehab before an operation, is because when a singer comes out of vocal surgery, their voice feels vulnerable and unsteady, so it can be overwhelming to introduce new singing and speaking techniques. There are too many other things to think about, too many worries to overcome. When possible, I always teach my clients the vocal technique necessary to put them on the path to vocal health *before* undergoing surgery, which means they will have more confidence moving forward into the next stage of their vocal rehab.

During our three weeks of pre-op work, I taught ⸄ about her SPA and how to engage and move through her Chest, Mix, and Head voices. We went over lowering her larynx when she sang and worked on eliminating her tendency to overcompensate for her weakened vocal cords by using the muscles in her neck—*Type A vocal personality*. One week prior to surgery, her doctor prescribed a week of full vocal rest. Her vocal cords got a much needed break before the surgical procedure. After the operation, she followed the doctor's recommendation of two weeks of vocal rest. Then, I was able to ease her back into training in order to bring her vocal cords back to strength and health—*physical fitness for the singer.*

After six post-operative weeks of rehabbing her vocal cords, 🎵 was hitting notes she had never hit before. During this time, she wrote two songs, back-to-back, with ranges far higher than she could ever have imagined singing before. When she sang the songs for the first time in my studio, she was so overcome with emotion and joy, tears streamed down her face. She had accomplished something she had thought impossible only two short months before. The surprise twist was her resistance to singing the song that had skyrocketed her to fame. She didn't like singing it anymore because it reminded her of a time of distress and imbalance in her life. But the song had legions of fans, and her new management team and I agreed that it made no sense to eliminate it from her setlist. We were going to have to find a way to make it work. 🎵 and I listened to the recording of the song at my studio. It sounded cool; her voice was raspy, angsty. Her old voice was all vocal fry, an alluring, scratchy sound, coveted and mimicked by many singers.

The rasp in 🎵's voice was a result of the cyst. Now she was healthy, the rasp was gone, and she didn't want to look back. With coaching and support, she was able to see her break-out, chart-topping single as an anthem of her resilience and ability to rise above a near devastating roadblock. We worked together to get her accessing those low notes with her full Chest voice, without engaging the muscles in her neck. In the end, she was able to enjoy the song again and overcome the demons that had plagued her.

Be careful of mimicking a sustained, raspy sound when singing or speaking. Consistently forcing your voice into a sound that isn't your natural voice puts extreme strain onto your SPA. It may sound cool, but it is a dangerous and unsustainable practice.

With both ♭ and ♮, I used simple warm-ups, arpeggios, increasingly difficult vowel sounds, and other techniques to bring them back to vocal health and balance. Proper vocal technique training is the solution to many vocal issues. I have been teaching for more than two decades, and I have never had a client who is plugged-in and working with me, develop a vocal injury. *Not on my watch.* We all know celebrity singers who have developed vocal injuries requiring surgeries and extensive vocal rest that put huge speed bumps in their careers. If they had a better understanding of their SPA and how to use it, they could have avoided these injuries and would not have gone through the physical and emotional stress.

BEHIND THE SCENES: FROM TONSILLECTOMY TO THE TOP

♯ was referred to me when she was ready to start live shows and touring. She had already broken record sales with more than four singles and was finally ready to hit the road with her live show. She had a very good voice, great pitch and tone, but she was struggling with achieving a fuller sound. With a habit of pulling her Chest voice hard at her bridge, she knew that the live element of performing was going to take its toll.

64

VOCAL CHECK-UP TIME

We had our first meeting over FaceTime, which isn't an optimal setting for assessment, but when you are dealing with huge artists, their grueling schedules are back-to-back, so an in-person lesson can be tricky. ♯ had been a singer and actor since childhood and sang well because of it, however, I immediately noticed she had a loss of power and range due to a lack of proper technical training. It's one thing to record an album with tuning, melodyne, background and stacking vocals with all the bells and whistles. It's quite a different story for a singer to perform night after night, live on TV, in large arenas, indoors and out. Throw in travel through changing time zones, health issues, vocal fatigue, lack of sleep, late nights, with the added challenges of personal life, and living the dream can quickly become an artist's worst nightmare.

I started straight away with some phonation exercises which she had never attempted before. These made an immediate improvement in her use of her vocal cords, rather than the muscles in her neck, to get through her first bridge. We then moved to low larynx exercises and modified vowels. ♯ is an excellent student, as she is extremely disciplined and takes direction well. There was no ego, only eagerness to learn, making our relationship as teacher and student an excellent fit.

We had to jump straight into rehearsals for two of the biggest award shows in the music business. We had just three weeks to prepare for her first live performance. I recall her being understandably nervous, but with the right training, I knew in my heart that she would not only pull it off, but deliver a sensational show. We did our routine drills, in addition to an exercise which taught her how to place her voice in the Mix to float her vocals with ease, showing no signs of struggle. We jumped straight into massive rehearsals with a full band, not to mention the added pressure of a documentary being filmed simultaneously, (as many artists do these days).

What the public would never know, was that all the while, she was dealing with severe tonsillitis, which simply could not be addressed until five months later, once her live shows were complete. Thankfully, not only did she perform beautifully, we were able to hone her technique with such precision, she made it through her live shows, swollen tonsils and all, without any issues.

The next step in our journey would be crucial to her future as a singer. I referred her to one of LA's top Laryngologists for surgery to remove the tonsils. Any surgical procedure can be daunting, especially one involving the throat of a professional singer. Tonsillectomy for an adult is quite painful, but the surgery went smoothly and ♯ took every precaution to ensure a good recovery. The fact that she had worked so hard to retrain her SPA prior to her operation, made her healing time much quicker.

We next had the task of rehabilitating ♯ after she began to heal. The holidays had come and gone and the touring season was upon us, so time was of the essence. I worked with her on phonation, placement, and vowel modification, slowly placing more pressure on her vocal cords, much like gradually adding weight to a barbell in the gym. Her schedule demanded that we pick up the pace with rehearsals, so we were careful to make sure she did not aggravate the healing process, by singing smart, not hard.

Within a month, we were preparing for the Grammys.

Not only did ♯ give a stellar live performance, but she walked away with not one, but her hands full of Grammy awards, including 'Best Vocals'. I could not have been more proud. I will never forget one of the most meaningful moments in my life as a vocal coach that night. As we stood together back-stage, ♯ leaned over and said, "These are your awards, too, Val. I could have never done this without you."

This is why I teach… this is what I love; watching an artist achieve their personal best, whether at home for the joy of it, in the recording studio, on a Broadway stage, on a TV show, in a movie, or side-stage at the Grammys, turning nominations in to gold.

♯ still trains with me to this day, because top athletes never stop seeking ways to improve their game. As artist, sculptor, painter, architect and poet, Michelangelo, said at the peak of his career, "I am still learning." ♯ embodies this philosophy and is an absolute joy to work with. I cannot wait to see how many more wonderful accomplishments she will achieve with her music and her voice.

If you have been diagnosed with a vocal injury and have discussed with your doctor the appropriate methods of treatment, you can begin your healing by doing some basic speech therapy exercises once you have been cleared to do so by your doctor, after completing any prescribed vocal rest. I do not recommend attempting vocal rehab by yourself. Contact a vocal coach technician with a track record of successfully rehabilitating singing voices.

REPROGRAM YOUR SPA

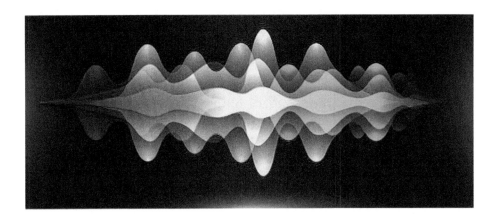

"The exercises and tips vocal tips Valerie has given me have made singing more fun, more relaxed. Her scientific and personal approach really worked for me. She's taught me ways of using my voice that have helped my pitch, phrasing, and clarity, without altering my personal style. She has really turned me on to the joy of singing."

—Jeff Bridges, Actor

Maybe you have tried to tackle one of your most challenging songs, only to find yourself struggling to sing through those difficult lines. Why? Because you may be lacking the essential building blocks of the foundation necessary to strengthen your voice. All of the tools and techniques I use with my students are essential to understanding and strengthening the SPA, but the most important thing to remember is: *singing is about balancing air flow and muscle.* Learning to manipulate the sounds we make to ensure our SPA maintains this balance of air flow and muscle is the key to successfully singing confidently through the toughest songs. But as this next story shows, finding that balance is not always easy.

BEHIND THE SCENES: MAKING THE IMPOSSIBLE POSSIBLE

Late one afternoon in the middle of summer, I received a call from ♩, the frontman of a multi-platinum rock band. One of my clients, who I had worked with during her world tour, referred him to me. ♩ told me that he had a tour in the Fall and was hoping we could work together to get him prepped and ready. I didn't know until we met a few days later, just how great a challenge he was facing.

When he walked into my vocal studio he presented as the classic bad boy. Disheveled clothing, tattoos and piercings, and rough around the edges. He had been training with another high-profile vocal coach but was still struggling. Before I took him through my vocal diagnostic, he opened up to me about his battle with alcoholism and how a resulting near-death experience drove him to sobriety. He had been touring with his band for over a decade, but this would be the first time he would be doing it sober. He was terrified and I was skeptical. Would he be willing to do the work necessary to get him singing his best before his first scheduled tour date?

REPROGRAM YOUR SPA

By the end of our first session, my skepticism vanished. It was clear that in spite of appearances, his heart and mind were ready to work. As he sang through my vocal diagnostic, it quickly became clear that he was Type A vocal personality—aggressively muscling his way across his vocal breaks. I put together a program of tailored warm-ups for him, and we spent the next few weeks balancing his vocals and training his SPA to move easily through the Chambers of his voice. Only once he had mastered those tools did we begin to work through his set list to pinpoint the challenging sections and strategize tools to sail through them.

♩ was a bit confused when I recommended the well-known Linkin Park's "In the End" to start working on his set list. It wasn't one of his songs or even in his repertoire. I explained to him that often when I am working with a singer who has songs that they have been performing for years, I will have them first tackle songs written and performed by other artists who have similar musical styles. This serves two purposes. One, it allows the singer to step away from any pre-programmed habits in their own music, so we can focus on re-programming and integrating new techniques. Two, it takes away the emotional attachment that the singer has to their original music. They don't have to feel like they are performing their songs for me but instead have the freedom to just sing, while tackling new tools and techniques. ♩'s songs demanded tremendous energy and volume, but since his health scare and sobriety, he had been afraid to open up and press into his vocals. "In the End" helped us work through those roadblocks step by step.

71

As ♩ sang through the song, we noted where he was having difficulty. Not surprisingly, the challenges were in the parts of the song where there were sustained notes over ♩'s vocal breaks. Once we knew where the challenges were, we began to dismantle them piece by piece. I took him back through a difficult section, but instead of singing the lyrics, I had him sing it only using the sound **Bub** on each note. We had been using an arpeggio (a broken chord in which individual notes are struck one by one, rather than all together at once) on **Bub**, in his vocal exercise program. That sound had helped him to lower his larynx so he could project with volume without straining. Singing through the challenging passage of the song using the **Bub** sound had the same effect. ♩ was blown away. What had felt impossible only seconds before, now felt free and easy.

About a minute into Linkin Park's, "In the End", one of the most challenging sections begins. The chorus is sung at a vocal break in the male voice, and the lyric, "I tried so hard..." uses sounds that engage ♩'s tendencies towards Type A vocal personality. The *a* and *r* in the word *hard* made him sing too broadly, which forced his larynx to rise and squeeze his vocal cords, which made for a painful experience for ♩'s SPA...*and my ears!* So, to counteract all the forces working against a pitch perfect and strain free vocal moment, I had ♩ sing the sound **Hud** instead of articulating *hard.* By modifying the vowel from *ah* to *uh* and eliminating the *r* consonant, ♩ could use the vowel sounds that helped him through his warm-ups to keep his larynx in a neutral position. The audience don't hear the difference, because the word still comes across as *hard,* but we transformed his vocal experience with that one small modification. By cheating that vowel a little, ♩ found himself singing easily, without muscle strain.

♩ and I worked through the song word by word, identifying the areas where vowel modifications were needed. For his voice, we modified the word **end** and had him sing **und** instead. On the word *really*, we changed the vowel sound from *re-lee* to *re-lay*. Often times we would have to go back to switching-out the lyric to the **Bub** sound before bringing the modified vowel lyric back. Each time we chipped away at his old bad habits and cemented the new techniques into his vocal experience. This is a rewarding and effective approach, and after working through "In the End," ♩ was thrilled and ready to tackle one of his own hit songs.

Not surprisingly, when he started singing his own music, some of his bad vocal habits resurfaced. We used the same tools, by switching out his lyrics with **Bub** and **Gug**, and slowly reintroducing lyrics little by little. By modifying vowels as needed until his SPA was locked into the new techniques, he was soon singing with freedom and ease.

We worked together like this for about six weeks before his tour. ♩ proved himself to be a great client—one of the hardest working and most determined I have ever had the pleasure to coach. Before he set off on the road, he knew how to sing freely through his Chest, Mix, and Head voices. His breaks had turned into smooth bridges, and his Mix voice was now as strong and confident as his Chest and Head voices. He was singing with the volume and power his songs required without any strain. Those six weeks were a transformative experience for him. He couldn't believe what he was feeling in his body. During one of our final pre-tour sessions together, we were working easily through a song that had once been a voice destroyer for him, and ♩ turned to me with a look of amazement and said, "That was full voice and I didn't even feel it." He not only knew the tools he needed, but how to implement them into his songs— he had reprogrammed his SPA. That feeling is nirvana for the singer.

BEHIND THE SCENES: GOING TO THE NEXT LEVEL

♫♫ came to my studio with several hit songs under his belt and a ferocious drive to push himself as far and as hard as he could. He told me he was ready for his vocals to be as invincible as possible. He wanted to be able to sing all the greats from Sam Cooke to Aretha Franklin, and he was ready to work for it. Unfortunately, ♫♫ had partied hard during the years his songs were charting, and he had spent almost all of his fortune. Regardless, he wanted to invest in his voice and was determined to cover as much ground as possible.

We agreed to meet three times a week for an initial three months. This was an ambitious schedule, but I soon learned ♫♫ was more than up to the task. We began, as I always do, with the Five Tone Ah diagnostic. He had a good voice and the potential to be great. I took him through the arpeggio exercises for his voice, and he took to them quickly, feeling the change in his voice, which made him even more motivated. In between our sessions, he committed himself to practicing the exercises at home. In the span of just a few short weeks, his voice became exponentially more powerful and his range had grown so much that he began to change how and what he was writing. He wrote a song that showcased his new abilities and range—it had a great hook and was catchy as hell. But instead of recording the song himself, he decided to sell it to another artist, knowing it would get more play and have a greater shot at success. He was right. The money started coming in again and he doubled down on his time with me. ♫ reprogrammed his SPA and mastered the arpeggio exercises faster than any client I had ever had. He was a perfectionist with a fierce desire to learn.

BEHIND THE SCENES: A SUSTAINED HIGH

Vibrato is one of the most misunderstood tools that many believe is a sound best left to opera singers. It's actually a tool that strengthens your voice and helps you stay on pitch, especially on sustained notes in the higher registers. I have a lot of successful artists who have never had vibrato.

One such client was rock star, ♪. He was a great singer but he had difficulty sustaining a note for any length of time without going off pitch. I told him it was because he wasn't using vibrato, but he resisted learning vibrato for weeks, because he feared it would change his highly marketable sound. I finally assured him I had never changed a singer's tone. The tools I teach make my singers bionic so they can still sound like themselves night after night, while maintaining a healthy SPA. It took some practice, but he eventually came around to understanding the value of this useful vocal tool.

Some months after he left on tour, I received a message from ♪ saying,

"Not only do I understand the importance of vibrato, I'm now using it in my shows."

Whenever I say *vibrato* to a new client, they have a similar aversion, because they assume I'm going to try to get them to sound like opera and classical musical theater singers. I would agree that operatic and musical theater teachers can be dangerous for rock and pop artists, since many times their students come out of sessions sounding overly trained, losing the rawness that first captured their fan base. Because of this, there are a lot of labels and managers out there who are wary of vocal teachers. Vibrato, when taught properly, is a really useful tool to improve flexibility, power, and sustainability.

Vibrato gets the vocal cords moving very, very rapidly, which creates a vibration and balanced airflow that strengthens and relaxes your vocal cords to help you sustain a note on pitch. Sustaining a note on a straight tone often causes the voice to wander off the pitch if the vocal cords are not strong enough, because it locks them up. If a singer doesn't use vibrato much in their songs, then I introduce vibrato solely as a training exercise—similar to football players running through tires on the field. The vibrato strengthens their vocal cords, so when they go back to singing their songs they can more easily sustain notes on a straight tone while using a small bit of what I call a *ghost vibrato*, (the tiniest bit of vibrato), to stay on pitch by keeping their vocal cords flexible.

Vibrato will make your vocal muscles faster, stronger, and more agile. You are not going to advance yourself as a singer without it. Like ♪, vibrato might not be part of your singing style, and you have no intention of using it much in your performance. It is true that many pop and rock singers hardly use vibrato. But let us return to the football analogy. The players don't run through tires during a game, but doing the exercise during practice will make them more effective on the field. Regardless of whether or not you intend to use vibrato in your music, every singer needs to use it in their vocal exercises. My clients and I always end up cracking up laughing while doing vibrato, but it works. Most of my clients nail their vibrato within a few short months. I have had clients with a dead straight tone who come in thinking they cannot do it, and I have always been able to get them there. By the time they have mastered it, all of my singers love using vibrato. My heavy metal and hard core rock artists put it best when they say it makes them "even more badass". Yes, it does.

Towards the end of our three months together, ♪ was vocally bionic. He could sing Aretha Franklin's version of "Bridge Over Troubled Water", *in her key*. He could sing Sam Cooke in a way that would make Sam, himself, proud. He wrote another chart-topping hit and was nominated for a Grammy. After our series of sessions were complete, he went on a national tour that later expanded into Europe. Not once did he experience any vocal issues. Watching him grow into the artist he had dreamed of becoming was tremendously rewarding.

BREATH OF LIFE

While breathing is often the first thing some voice coaches discuss with their students, for me, it almost always comes last. I typically only introduce this topic with my advanced clients who find that they want even more power behind their voices, typically a hard rock or opera singer. Breathing is an advanced tool, because you will sing more freely if you can relax, but if you are focused on how you are breathing you are more likely to become tense. I almost always balance the SPA first, through targeted vocal warm-ups, vowel modifications, vibrato and transferring muscle energy, because then, adding breath control techniques can be effective, if they are taught properly.

I have heard so many stories from singers who have studied with other teachers who encourage belly breathing or talk about singing from the diaphragm without an ability to effectively explain what that means. I ask those clients what they learned from those breathing techniques. The answer I always hear is that it did nothing to improve their vocal experience. It didn't work. Nine times out of ten, they will say that it made them feel more tense. This happens because focusing on breathing creates imbalance in the SPA, because your diaphragm is a far stronger muscle than your vocal cords. For example, let's say your vocal cords can withstand two pounds of pressure while your diaphragm can handle a whopping fifty pounds. If you are focusing on controlling and strengthening the diaphragm instead of strengthening your vocal cords, then you are asking for trouble. Think of it like bench-pressing. If you put two pounds of weight on one side of the bar for the vocal cords, and then you put fifty pounds on the other side for the diaphragm, what's going to happen? The whole thing is going to topple over. There is no balance.

When a teacher starts talking about breathing too soon, it confuses the singer because they are being taught to think of air being in the belly and diaphragm, but the air is not in the belly at all. Then, the singer is asked to push out too much air with too much force through their delicate vocal cords, without the benefit of understanding how to regulate that air. The result is an overtaxed and imbalanced SPA. Breathing exercises can easily create unnecessary tension in the voice.

Instead, I always encourage my clients to **not** think about breathing when they sing. For example, babies can cry for days and not lose their voice—they are not thinking about controlling their breath, they are just letting the sound happen. Pop singers should just breathe normally, and introduce proper ribcage breathing techniques when they have balanced their SPA.

There are always exceptions to this. Sometimes a client will come into my studio who is always out of breath when they sing, or is holding their breath. The reason for this is usually nerves, creating tension in the SPA and body, and/or because they are trying to breathe into their stomach or raising their shoulders when taking a breath. I will stop my vocal diagnostic and explain that their breathing issue is primarily due to nerves and stomach/shoulder breathing causing tension, which is why it is important we work on the vocal exercises to relax their SPA and body.

Top Left: Post-Grammy win with Olivia Rodrigo
Middle: LipRoll podcast with Bishop Briggs
Bottom: Training Kelvin Harrison Jr. for "Mufasa" in "The Lion King" prequel

Top Left: At home training Tom Ellis **Top Right:** Recording with Tom Ellis for "Lucifer"
Bottom: Tom Ellis on LipRoll podcast

Top Left: Getting Rita Wilson ready for Disney Concert Hall **Top Right:** Training Jayden Hossler for upcoming tour **Bottom Left:** Working on "Pitch Perfect" movie set with Harvey Mason Jr. **Bottom Right:** Working with David Bowie and Abbey Road

Top: At home with Debbie Gibson and Joely Fisher

Bottom: In Beijing with Avril Lavigne

Festival Time with Noah Cyrus

Warming up for "Jimmy Kimmel Live!"

Top: LipRoll podcast with Reeve Carney
Bottom: In studio with Ozzy Osbourne

Top: Recording with The Chainsmokers in London
Bottom: Fit body Fit voice

LipRoll Podcast with client Joe Buck

On tour with Drew Taggart and The Chainsmokers

Top: In Vegas warming up Rascal Flatts
Bottom: In studio with Mike Posner

Top Left: Working on "Nashville" on CBS **Top Right:** At the "Grand Ole Opry" with Connie Britton **Bottom:** Hanging with the cast and crew of "Nashville"

Top: LipRoll podcast with Nico and Vinz
Middle: LipRoll podast with Ryan Cabrera **Bottom:** Festival fun with Labrinth

Top: LipRoll podcast with Judith Hill
Bottom: Pre-show warm-ups with Luke Hemmings of 5SOS

Top: LipRoll podcast with Scout Willis
Bottom Left: Working with "T-Bone" Burnett on "Nashville"
Bottom Right: In studio with Sidney Sierota of Echosmith

Festival time with Jordan McGraw

Working in studio with Lesley-Ann Brandt of "Lucifer"

Tour rehearsals and backstage with 5SOS

Top: In studio with Alec Benjamin
Bottom: In studio with Sum 41's Deryck Whibley

TAKING YOUR VOICE TO THE NEXT LEVEL

"I would not be the singer I am today without Val. She changed my voice and the way I sing for the better, and I'm grateful to be her student."

—Luke Hemmings, 5 *Seconds of Summer*

As a vocal coach, I always take time to learn more about the voice. I regularly meet with the voice doctors I collaborate with, and I love finding out about the new techniques and advances in medicine to help the voice. I also appreciate that these doctors are open to discussing the successes I have with strengthening my clients' voices. Learning is an essential part of continuing to grow, and I pass that onto all my clients—whether they come in to heal their voices, develop their instrument, or for a quick fix. No matter how advanced someone's voice gets, there are always ways to switch it up and take it to the next level.

Every now and then I meet a new client whose voice is already strong and just needs a few adjustments to take them where they want to go to. They easily run through the basic warm-ups and catch onto the new tools quickly. I can tell that their voice is ready for more advanced warm-ups and tools. Teaching is all about listening and adjusting my program to the client I have in front of me. The stories below were no exception.

BEHIND THE SCENES: FAST LEARNER

It was late summer several years ago, when I got a call from a manager friend of mine. He had a client, one of the biggest pop singers in the world, who was looking for a new vocal coach. had reached a plateau with her current teacher and was hungry for a change. She was even more motivated to start fresh because she was staring down the road at a world tour. Due to a combination of fatigue and poor technique, she was having a hard time singing through her set. I agreed to meet with her at her home to see how I could help. Only a few short days later, I arrived at her imposingly large home in Bel Air and rang the bell, expecting a member of her staff to answer. But, much to my surprise, greeted me at the door and welcomed me inside. We walked down several hallways before arriving at a room, the centerpiece of which was a beautiful grand piano.

I sat down at the piano and asked her about her voice and what issues she was struggling with, in order to get a better sense of what we were facing. We hadn't been talking for too long before I had 🎤 dive in and sing through some scales. Tonally, she had the coolest sound. I could immediately hear that she was straining to use her Chest voice when she should have been singing from her Mix. Her Head voice, on the other hand, was nice, if a little weak and breathy. I took her through the basic warm ups and discovered that she had only two gears. She either sang really loudly and strained, or was very breathy—*Type A and Type B combined*. For her brand of pop music, that would never fly in live performance, especially on an intense, headlining world tour.

I had to get 🎤 to start releasing all of the muscle tension that was driving her bad vocal habits by having her focus on Running Arpeggios on **Bub, We,** and **Loo,** so she could find her Mix. When we came across an issue with singing through her vocal breaks, we paused to talk about vowel modifications. She proved to be a fast learner, and we were about thirty minutes into our hour session when she had an epiphany. She began to feel how the changes in vowel sounds coupled with the focusing on her Mix voice gave her a greater sense of ease in her vocals without a loss of power. We pushed on. I knew she was one of those singers who was both Type A (strain) and Type B (breathy), so I needed to find the right balance of exercises to address her opposing issues. I took her through a Running Arpeggio on the sound **Gee**. The **Gee** sound encourages more cord closure, but it still puts the larynx into a low or neutral position. Then she nailed the Running Arpeggio on this vowel sound right away. Most people take three or four sessions to move through the kinds of exercises we tackled together in one hour. ⌢ asked me some very specific questions about what was happening in her SPA. She was a hungry for more knowledge.

This was our first session, and I wanted her to feel the potential of what was to come, so we jumped ahead into one of her songs. ⌢ was several albums into a career that had made her millions. High energy artists at the top of their game don't want to wait to implement the tools they are learning, so it's important to me that they feel like they are succeeding so they will be encouraged to continue doing the work.

After our first pass through the song, it became clear where her issues were. For starters, she wasn't able to do the vocal run that was at the heart of her song, and I could see she was frustrated. It was imperative to me that I get her through the vocal run successfully. I had her sing the run on a **Bub**, a neutral vowel that was her easiest warm-up word, however, it wasn't so easy for her in the context of the song. So I had her sing it on a **Bob** instead. It lowered her larynx just enough to place her voice in the Mix. Once she felt the correct placement and her vocals clicked into place, we reintroduced the lyric, while modifying the vowels as necessary to get her larynx low and her confidence high. It worked beautifully.

Finally, I asked her to pull up a chair and *lean into it* on the high note. The combination of transferring muscle energy into the chair, modifying the vowel, and lowering the larynx made it possible for her to hit the notes like it was nothing. The experience for her was night and day from where she had begun only sixty minutes before. She felt it, *she got it*. That moment was a total physical and emotional revelation. She looked at me and said, "Where have you been my whole career? You're my vocal coach. Period." Over the next several weeks I continued to move her quickly through a series of increasingly difficult vocal exercises. By the second or third session I introduced the Short Arpeggio with Repeat, the Short Arpeggio with Repeat and Sustain, and the Broken Arpeggio.

Shortly after our first few sessions, ⌢ and I were traveling the world together on her tour. Our tour routine looked something like this: I would go to her hotel room a few hours before the show and spend half an hour warming her up. She would then travel to the venue, do her meet and greets, sound checks, and final hair and makeup, before spending another twenty minutes with me backstage running arpeggios and making sure her voice was warmed up and ready to tackle the next two hours on stage. After about eight or nine songs, we would work together again backstage for a few short minutes to reposition her voice so that she could tackle the songs that were in a lower register. She was dedicated, worked hard, and the results were phenomenal. She sang for hours with very few mis-steps and without any auto-tune.

Throughout each show, I wore the belt pack the sound guy gave me, so her voice was constantly in my ear. I wrote notes on every single song—what worked, what didn't, and why. This kind of detailed analysis can sound overwhelming, but it was something 🔸 really appreciated. She was a perfectionist... *most of my artists are.*

🔸 wanted to know what she did not do well, but also what she nailed. Our close working relationship gave us a shorthand that allowed for a quick download of these observations at the end of the night. We met in her hotel room at the end of a long day, usually close to midnight, to go over my notes and answer any questions she had. We did all of this to reinforce the positive changes in her voice, and the tour continued to get better and more polished with each show. We worked like this for the next three weeks until 🔸 and I knew she had her vocals locked in for the next leg of her tour.

BEHIND THE SCENES: UNEXPECTED LESSON

Another very skilled artist I had the pleasure of working with came to me by way of a television producer. We had worked together on the *Nashville* series, where I was the vocal coach to the cast.

He admired the results I was getting from each of the actors on set and wondered if I would be willing to meet with a friend of his who was starting to show signs of struggling vocally. As it turned out, his friend had one of the most golden voices in the business and his twenty-year, chart-topping career was a testament to that. Of course, I agreed to meet with 🔹 and the other members of his band, so my friend made the arrangements. As it turned out, the arrangements were more complicated than I had anticipated. I was supposed to meet 🔹 backstage in Las Vegas right before their sold-out show. It was an opportunity I didn't want to pass up, so in spite of the imperfect set up, I agreed. When I arrived at the venue in Vegas, it became increasingly clear that ♮ was not expecting me.

I will admit that the whole situation was pretty uncomfortable, but I was determined to make a difference, even in this short window of time. I was ushered into a green room backstage where twenty or more of the band's close friends and family were hanging out. The guys walked in about an hour before curtain. They were in good spirits, but in no way interested in stopping the party in order to warm their voices with a complete stranger.

But... that was what I was there to do, so about forty minutes before showtime, I figured I would have to step up and make my presence known. I politely asked that the room be cleared so that the guys and I could get started. Thankfully, everyone listened. I could tell that ♮ was curious about me. My guess is he knew he needed help, but wasn't convinced yet that I was the person to do it. He packed his mouth with tobacco and settled in to see what I could do. The first thing I did was to ask him to take the tobacco out of his mouth—you cannot sing well with a cheek full of dip. He laughed and played nice, and we dug in.

I started the band with the basic warm-ups. ♮'s voice was as golden as his recordings had made it out to be, but there were a couple of sticking points. ♮ had never had a voice lesson in his life, so I had the daunting task of making this introduction to the world of vocal exercises as compelling and convincing as possible. I talked him through the SPA nitty gritty pretty quickly and then told him my goal was to help him stay bionic by elevating his strength and stamina during his performances. He joked a lot, but I knew it was all in good humor. could do amazing things with his voice, but over time, he had lost a little ground. Instead of being able to sustain notes with his familiar vibrato, he had taken to having to insert more and more vocal runs. To begin to address this loss of power, I took him through an arpeggio on **No**. Then, because I knew he was already an advanced singer, I leapt ahead and talked about the role of the diaphragm in inserting power into the vocal performance. By way of encouraging him to really lean in, I reminded him of his many fans, all of whom remembered his songs with sustains and not runs. I encouraged him to make this effort on their behalf. He was a quick study. He did arpeggios with the word **We**, and began to understand how to balance air flow and muscle in order to release and relax into his vocals.

To further coax his voice into the proper placement, I told him not to think of the work we were doing as singing, but instead, as just talking. He immediately made that mental shift and it had the desired effect. I noticed 's biggest problem was his rough transitions in and out of Chest voice. It lacked fluidity. I talked to him about how the exercises we were doing would, over time, help make those transitions as smooth as silk. Would he commit to warming up for even five minutes a day? He was willing to try, if the effort meant more balanced vocals, that would ultimately mean he wouldn't struggle on stage.

Finally, we turned our attention to one of his songs. As I often do with my clients, I asked him to sing the lyrics on the sound **Bub** and as he got higher up in the register, to turn the **Bub** sound into more of a **Bob**. His voice sailed through the challenging passage and ♮ had the lightbulb moment that turned the tide for him. I now had his full attention. We added the lyric back in, and I encouraged him to use the muscle memory from the **Bub** when singing the words. Then I challenged him again. I told him our next step would be to sing through that passage of the song a half step up. He balked and said, "That's as high as it goes". But I asked him to trust me, telling him it would be easier to sing the song where it was written if he could stretch himself a little with this exercise. He sang the higher notes on the **Bub** with ease. Then we brought the song back down to where it was written, and, as I had promised, he sang it effortlessly.

Normally, I would never push new clients this hard and fast. I prefer to ease them in, making sure each step is well understood and locked in before adding additional challenges. But, as his unexpected vocal coach, I had less than forty minutes to make an impact, so I knew I needed to give ♮ a crash course. Given what I had heard from his voice in the early minutes of our time together, I decided it was a pretty good bet that he would be able to rise to the challenge and succeed. As I thought, he felt the shifts in his voice very quickly and was hooked.

The band went on stage, and I put on my 'in-ears' and began furiously typing notes into my phone. As with all my clients, I took notes on what was working and what needed adjusting. ♮ caught my eye from the stage, and when he had a break in the set, he came over to where I was sitting to check-in. Things were going great, the warm-up had been transformative. He knew it and so did I. But, in spite of his great skill and our stellar first session, I told him there was still much more we could do to make his work on stage even easier. He took it all in then walked back out to center stage. At the end of the night, and I sat down together and I shared my notes and suggestions for next steps. He listened intently, asked great questions, and then invited me to join them for the duration of their tour. So began a working relationship and friendship that has been tremendously rewarding.

YOUR SPEAKING VOICE MATTERS TOO

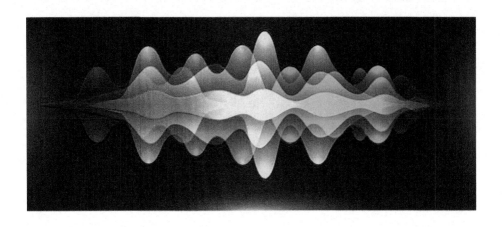

"Valerie Morehouse is a powerhouse. Her method not only evolved my singing voice, but transformed my speaking voice, which transformed my life."

—Mike Posner, Recording Artist

V ocal cord injuries do not discriminate based on profession. They are not exclusive to singers. They can affect anyone who uses their voice for a living. When I set out to teach singers to understand, strengthen, and heal their voices, my goal was to start singers on a path of vocal health to support them through tours, recording and press appearances. I never thought that my work would lead me into the world of public speakers, DJs, journalists, broadcasters, pastors, politicians, and more. But over time, my reputation for quickly and effectively rehabilitating damaged vocal cords spread into these professions. Screaming into the mic for hours at dance parties, speaking day in and day out on the campaign trail, delivering energetic sermons to large congregations week after week, or calling three-hour football games, also takes its toll on our delicate SPA. The good news is, speaking-related vocal issues can be resolved by using the same tools and techniques I use with my singers.

Rehabilitating the speaking voice should not be attempted alone. It is a very delicate balance of the correct exercises and guidance from a voice doctor and a vocal coach. Every voice has its own unique challenges, as you will see through the following three stories of a DJ, a sports caster, and a game show host.

BEHIND THE SCENES: A DJ

Being one of the top DJs in the world has it perks. Opportunities for vocal rest isn't one of them. ♩ was referred to me by one of the top voice doctors in Beverly Hills, someone I had collaborated with many times in the past. ♩ had been diagnosed with a cyst and a pretty good-sized hemorrhage on his right vocal cord. This type of injury is not painful, which is both a plus and a negative. We never want our voices to experience pain, but because ♩ didn't feel any pain, he was less motivated to seek help. He had pushed himself to the breaking point. As with most vocal injuries, early detection and correction can be the difference between an easy recovery or a surgical intervention, followed by weeks of vocal rest and rehabilitation.

VALERIE MOREHOUSE

By the time ♩ reached out to me, he was on the tail-end of a 255-day world tour. Night after night, he had stirred up audiences of thousands, whipping them into a frenzy with shouts of "Jump! Jump!" while spinning his signature heart-thumping dance mixes and beats. He had back to back shows in cities across the globe, from Dubai to Dublin, Ibiza to Vegas. In addition to his gigs, he was producing music for other artists and designing a product line. He had a work schedule more punishing than any other I had ever encountered. From the get-go, I could hear how much trouble he was in vocally. On the phone, his voice was harsh and strained. He told me that by the end of a long work night he had no voice left at all and had resorted to having crowd pumpers do most of the on-stage shouting for him. His career was at stake, and he was understandably panicked.

He came into my studio with an entourage, an electric energy from nearly a year of non-stop club dates, with barely any speaking voice. Even though he had produced several hit singles, I was surprised to find out he had never sung. It took a little convincing, but I knew the best way for me to assess his vocal issues and address his concerns was through the time tested vocal diagnostic I use with some of the world's greatest voices. So I asked him to sing the Five Tone Ah. Singing on pitch is not a prerequisite for undertaking this valuable exercise, but in spite of his objections, he sang pretty well. I now had a clear picture of what his road to recovery would look like.

After going through my vocal diagnostic and consulting with his doctor, we knew that surgery was his best option. His voice was so weak that we couldn't do much rehab work prior to his operation, but we collaborated for several weeks after in order to slowly rehab his voice back to health, singing every step of the way. For speakers, I use a combination of speech therapy and singing exercises, because I have found the most effective way to rehab an injured vocal cord is by activating those muscles through singing. The speaking voice lives primarily in one vocal Chamber—the face. Singing gives access to the whole voice because it takes the voice through the Chest, Mix, and Head voices, which increases flexibility and stamina.

Singing was the ideal way to begin on a necessary light and gentle approach for ♩. We started with a very specific warm-up program with lots of aspirate consonant exercises like **Bub**, to help close the vocal cords—absolutely no vowels, only Arpeggios. At first, when I introduced a new scale, his whole body cringed. He was in full fight or flight mode. Singing for a non-singer can be a pretty scary experience, even without an audience. Thankfully, ♩ regularly meditated, so we used some of those mind/body techniques during our sessions to help release tension.

I had him sing the warm-up scales on the **We** sound to release the tension in his neck as its more aspirate or breathy going against his tendency to strain or pull weight up. Over time, this eliminated the catches in his voice. We used the **Bub** sound until he stopped 'hiking up' his larynx. His confidence grew as he felt his voice grow stronger. As a side benefit, ♩'s musical knowledge grew. When we started, he didn't even know what a scale was, now he was able to sing through several octaves. This was thrilling for him, because he knew this new tool would increase his effectiveness as a music producer.

Given all the years of abuse on his SPA, we made remarkable progress in a short amount of time. But right when I thought we were ready to take it to the next step, ♩ stopped coming in for sessions. I have learned over my many years working with professional singers and speakers, that it is very difficult for them to prioritize their health. People who are that highly driven feel unsteady when they are not moving at warp speed. They can feel as though too much is at stake if they stop. After two months and only about seven sessions, ♩ decided his voice was ready, and he left on tour for a year. Because of his premature departure, I was not able to teach him how to speak and shout properly or engage his diaphragm when pumping up the crowds from the stage.

I worried about him a lot that year. I knew he had left his vocal rehab program too soon and was at risk of a major relapse. Occasionally, I heard from his team who said he needed my help, and we tried for months to get him back into my studio without success. It wasn't until his voice really started to go downhill again that ♩ had the wake-up call he couldn't ignore. He called me up and told me he was taking a month off and clearing his calendar to allow him to focus and really get it right this time.

We agreed to resume our work, only if this time, ♩ would agree to stay the course. When he returned to my studio, his vocal cords were tired and swollen, but he wasn't struggling nearly as much as he had been a year before. His saving grace during the tour was his dedication to his warm-ups. He did them diligently before each show and often invited some of his artist friends, celebrity clients, and guests to warm up with him backstage, posting the evidence on Instagram. We dove back into using the arpeggios to reinforce the connection between his Chest, Mix, and Head voices. In addition, the two biggest things I focused on teaching ♩ were how to use his speaking voice by placing the sound in his Mix voice rather than yelling from his throat, and how to support his voice on stage, by introducing breathing techniques for to expand his ribcage and engage his diaphragm for optimal support and power. We practiced his onstage 'yell'. No straining, no neck muscles, only a powerful, resonant voice. While working on his stage voice, we discussed microphone technique. It may seem obvious, but many DJs and performers often forget the role the microphone plays in their performances. Its purpose is to amplify the voice. This means you should never have to strain your voice to reach the decibel level of your dreams.

Once he had recovered some ground, I introduced more advanced vocal tools, including vibrato. He loved the feeling of sustaining a note on vibrato. To him, it felt like a massage for his vocal cords. ♩ finally understood the importance of keeping his SPA healthy, and he was hooked. He committed to learning everything he could about protecting and strengthening his voice before we both agreed he was ready to dive back into his high octane life, with confidence and a foundation of understanding that would keep him vocal injury free.

BEHIND THE SCENES: A SPORTSCASTER

Another of my non-singing clients also came to me on the recommendation of one of the most cutting-edge voice doctors in the country. ♪ has been a sports caster of the biggest sporting events in the country for the better part of the last two decades. ♪'s career required him to talk and travel a lot, which had started to take a toll on his voice. Then, to make matters exponentially worse, an issue during a surgical procedure, unrelated to his voice, had paralyzed his left vocal cord. He went to visit his voice doctor, who did a few procedures to help mobilize the cord, but it was clear ♪ also needed vocal rehabilitation.

Our initial meeting was a Skype call. I could immediately hear during our short conversation, that one vocal cord was not moving properly. We agreed to work together and during our first session, I started to run him through my vocal diagnostic. Unsurprisingly, ♪ was very reluctant to sing. This was very uncomfortable territory for him. I explained to him that singing was the best and quickest route to vocal health and returning to his career. Traditional speech therapy exercises are effective, but in my experience, they don't engage the three Chambers of the voice or engage the muscles in the vocal cords as effectively as focused singing exercises. I then played a few notes on the keyboard and discovered that ♪ actually has a really nice voice.

This kind of discovery always excites me, and usually it makes the client happy when they learn as an adult, that they actually have some musical ability. But this was not ♪'s reaction. From his perspective, in his line of work, singing exercises were very nearly taboo. ♪ did not want to sing, however, he accepted what I was saying about singing creating a faster path to his voice rehabilitation. He made it very clear from the start that he would not, under any circumstance, be singing in front of anybody but me, and he did not want anyone else to know that he sang. The singing we would do in my studio became the sports world's best kept secret. I kept ♪'s secret until he came on my podcast, **LipRoll**. Much to my surprise and delight, he shared this story and even sang during our chat!

♪ lived out of state and flew to Los Angeles to meet with me once or twice a month, with Skype sessions in between. By combining speech therapy exercises with my vocal rehabilitation program, I was able to guide him to place his voice properly in the Chambers of his voice rather than in his over-exerted neck muscles. I made good on my promise to have him sing his way out of this predicament. I used the arpeggios on different sounds so we could find the different pitches which he could resonate on. I even had him resonating in head voice which expanded his range as a speaker.

Just like singers, public speakers have a unique sound, and it absolutely vital they maintain it. The tone ♪ had, was a combination of his natural voice and a bad habit from his teenage years; one of pushing his throat to create a deeper sound, which was unnecessarily hurting and tiring his voice. During our sessions, we worked on recreating that deeper sound by moving the sound from his throat, to resonating through his Mix voice in his face. We were able to preserve his rich, warm tone, only now when he spoke, there was no more strain, only a resonant and sustainable sound.

To continue to increase the strength, flexibility and stamina of his SPA, I had him sing through entire songs. He opted to try the classic Eagles anthem, "Desperado". The irony of the title was not lost on either of us. He was putting his career in my hands, and it was a decidedly vulnerable position. In the end, ♪'s leap of faith paid off. His vocal cord recovered and his voice came back as rich and recognizable as ever. By using vocal warm-ups and songs, we were able to rehabilitate him at three times the pace of traditional speech therapy. Several months later, I received a text from him as he was preparing to announce a major sporting event. He thanked me for helping him through that difficult time. His voice was back in the game and stronger than ever.

BEHIND THE SCENES: A GAME SHOW HOST

Sometimes a client will come to me on the day of an important speech or televised event, needing immediate solutions in order to get through the gig. This was the case with ♪. He was hosting a game show and was in Los Angeles shooting two episodes daily. He called me and said he was crashing at the end of each day. I could hear that his vocal cords were healthy and that the issue was more about voice placement. ♪ knew he wasn't getting it right, but he didn't know how to fix it. He came into my studio, and we had one hour to cover everything. I took him on the fast track through the same speech exercises that I used with ♪: Lip Rolls, hands up while saying energy words—*the whole toolkit*. His voice began to relax, and he could start to feel the proper sound placement, so I introduced breath control techniques and diaphragm use for speakers. Breathing is very important for speakers because their voice primarily lives in one vocal Chamber. Breathing exercises that engage the diaphragm help them move sound to the face and away from the throat. By engaging his diaphragm, he felt even more secure in placing the sound in his face, so we started adding phrases in the script of the game show. My hour session with ᴧᴧ was intense and a quick fix, but it worked. The next afternoon, I got a text from him, after he wrapped the second show of the day, saying he felt amazing and his voice wasn't tired at all. In fact, he felt as though he could have tackled two more. That's what I call a win!

TAKING CARE OF YOUR VOICE: PART 1
MIND GAMES

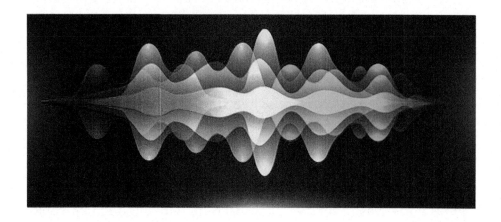

"I've tried every voice coach from Los Angeles to New York; Valerie's teaching style is the only one that makes sense to me."

—**Avril Lavigne,** Singer/Recording Artist

My studio is located in the heart of Los Angeles. It is a city with a reputation for an obsessive fixation with health and fitness. Fad diets live and die here, and new workout regimes are adopted by what can only be described as blind faith. To say that it is difficult to separate fact from fiction in Hollywood, is the understatement of the century. If you ever do a Google search for your favorite artist's diet and exercise programs, you will usually be met by a barrage of contradictory and unsustainable suggestions. But what does it really take to be one of the world's top vocal artists? How do you take care of yourself and your instrument so that you can produce an incredible sound, night after night, that will wow your audiences, while keeping you energized, healthy, and singing your best? The answer has less to do with what you eat and how you exercise (although this kind of self-care is important), and everything to do with how you think and feel about yourself. One of my greatest challenges as a vocal coach is to help untie the emotional knots that stop my clients' voices from shining.

For these stories, I use the names **Anon,** aka *anonymous*, and **Incog,** aka *incognito*, because they are based on the combined experiences of **many** artists who have come through my door, and do not identify any one artist. Mental health is incredibly private and important. It's not my place to share each person's individual story, rather, these stories reflect the collective pain and frustrations my clients and I have faced together, *and conquered*. They are **all of us**!

BEHIND THE SCENES: FINDING JOY AGAIN

Anon had an extremely successful career and had been nominated *and won,* multiple awards over the years. But in the middle of a national tour, his vocal performances began to degrade, and no one could figure out why. He was fit and healthy, with no obvious vocal injuries, and yet, still he struggled to get through his set list, or hit notes that used to be well within his reach. He worked hard for years with another vocal coach without seeing any improvements. By the time he came into my studio to meet with me, he was clearly at the end of his rope.

Anon arrived in my studio with swagger, yet beneath his charismatic persona was an undercurrent of uncertainty and vulnerability. More often than not, when a singer is having issues with their singing voice, their speaking voice will show evidence of the strain…but not **Anon**. His speaking voice was healthy and bright. There was something more to this persistent vocal mystery.

I started to run him through the Five Tone Ah and it became evident very quickly that he had **vocal dysphonia**, a disorder that causes a lack of coordination in the vocal cords, which sounds like a disruption, or nervous flutter in the voice, when they sing or speak. The tension can cause the voice to be pitchy and to have difficulty transitioning through the Chambers of the voice. The cause of this can be emotional distress, physical damage, or sometimes both. Everything in his SPA was squeezing and pinching rather than opening and flowing. He had lost all of his Mix voice and was overusing his Chest voice—bringing it up way too high, which caused his larynx to choke him out. He also had massive vocal breaks and no control of his instrument, so at times he wasn't singing on key. This was terrifying for him. He had an album coming out and a tour to prepare for, all while trying desperately to hide his vocal issues. Despite it seeming like a visceral issue, it was clear to me that there was nothing physically wrong with his voice. Instead, after listening to him talk about his fears and frustrations, I could tell he was carrying a heavy emotional burden, and *this* was the root of his issue.

Singers are artists. And as artists, we are often more connected to our emotions. Our life's work is to dig deep and bare our souls, to connect our audience to something bigger than all of us. So what happens when we become afraid, no longer believing in our talent? When we lose confidence in ourselves and self-doubt sets in, over time we can begin to see physical manifestations of our emotional tumult. If we pretend that everything is perfect while our world crumbles inside of us, we will end up getting buried under a pile of rubble, letting ourselves believe that we have become ineffective or irrelevant.

In **Anon's** case, his physical issues were driven by an emotional fear of becoming obsolete. Scales and vocal tools alone were not going to fix this problem. *So we talked.* His managers and producers had made efforts to reinvent his image, pushing him further out of his comfort zone and away from his truth. His whole life had become about pleasing other people, so he stopped asking, and being asked, what *he* wanted. This is very dangerous for an artist. Our truth is who we are. When we deny it in order to please someone or to chase something, we are setting ourselves up for a fall. **Anon** had lost sight of himself and he was emotionally rattled and out of control. Thankfully, he began to trust me and open up as I coached him through tools to help him identify the positive, meditate on it, breathe with mindful intention, and repeat.

We supported his emotional recovery by working on reversing the ingrained bad habits in his voice by focusing on the foundational basic warm-ups. As he learned to relax his larynx and sing through his

Chest, Mix, and Head voices, his confidence also improved. But **Anon's** would not be a quick recovery. When an emotional or physical issue is not addressed when it first occurs, it becomes much more complicated to resolve. **Anon** was no different than anyone else who finds themselves in this position. He wanted to know how long it would take to get his vocals back on track. I didn't have an answer, and I rarely do, because it truly is different for everyone. I was, however, able to assure him that he would get steadily better. I ask my clients to commit to the process, moving forward step by step, rather than attaching themselves to the outcome. I asked **Anon** to do the same.

Over the next several months, we worked together through some of his live shows and recording sessions, and every time, I did my part to remind him how well he was doing. Surrounding him with positive reinforcement was very important. He had to shield himself from the naysayers. During recovery, the last thing he needed around him were negative people. I encouraged him to find the people who loved and supported him… and stick with them.

Anon improved steadily, and after a full year of dedicated practice, he wrote to me while on tour, to say that *he was back*! His musical director and managers also called me to share the good news of how incredible he was sounding. **Anon** was over the moon with happiness and gratitude. He was able to sing from the bottom of his Chest voice, through his Mix, and into his Head voice and back down, without struggling. He continued to sing with ease through an entire year on tour and beyond.

YOUR TURN: YOUR EMOTIONAL JOURNEY

When a client walks into my studio, I take stock of many things, not the least of which is how they carry themselves. What energy are they bringing into the room? What baggage is following them around? Quiet and shy, effervescent and funny, these can all be authentic representations of who they are, or they can be very effective coping mechanisms, masking a bigger emotional problem. My job is to not only figure out their vocal strengths and weaknesses, but to uncover what emotional issues the client may be facing. No warm-up plan is complete without tools to help the artist on their emotional journey. If you want to be an artist, then you need to be prepared to dig deep into your emotional life, where the good, and *not so good* stuff lies. You will be a more effective performer if you can connect with your emotions rather than just trying to sound good. Like most athletic endeavors, singing is as much an emotional mind game as it is a physical one.

Sometimes, I will encounter a singer who is so scared, that they sing with their mouths nearly closed. They are usually in denial that deep down they are actually scared to be heard and even defend their raspy, muffled tone as their *unique* sound, when in reality, it's just a collection of their weaknesses.

Some singers hide behind trying to sound like someone else. They make terrific karaoke singers, but that's it. There is nothing personal or emotional in their performances, nothing that makes it ring true or break through. Their act is robotic, because there is nothing of *them* in it. These are just two of the many emotional obstacles I come across while teaching, but they usually all come back to some kind of fear.

Singing is never just about training your voice and understanding your SPA. It is also about your heart, mind, and soul. You have to have a story to tell. You have to be willing to tap into your vulnerabilities. There is a difference between being a singer, *and being an artist*. If you want to sell records, you have to be willing to tap into your heart, as well as your mind, in order to expose your emotional core. Even if you are singing a cover, you have to understand where the person was coming from when they wrote that song, then transfer it into your own experience, to make it your own. This is the art. If you do not have the right intention and energy behind your singing, then your listeners will feel something is a little off. They will never truly become a part of the experience. They will never understand the story you are trying to tell, because you haven't figured out the story for yourself.

POSITIVE AFFIRMATIONS & MINDFUL BREATHING

If you realize there are emotional roadblocks preventing you from finding your true voice and negatively affecting your singing, then it is important for you to know that this is a very common concern for many professional singers, and you must be patient. These are not quick fixes, but they work if you put in the time and commit yourself to the process. Here are two suggestions you can use to begin to free yourself and your voice.

Start by trying to identify the moment when things began going downhill for you vocally. When did you first feel a change in your voice? When did things start going south? Was it something someone said to you that triggered a lasting and spiralling self-doubt? Was it a negative script you wrote for yourself? Once you have pinpointed the reason or reasons that started your vocal decline, then you can begin to discredit the old storyline that isn't serving you and begin to write a new, positive story for yourself.

The next step is to identify at least five things you like about your voice and musical talent. This is no time for modesty—no one will read this list but you. Do you like the tone of your voice? Are you proud of your range? Do you love the songs you write? Whatever it is, write it down and keep this list somewhere you can access every day.

Commit to reading this list of positive attributes out loud, every single day, ideally right before you begin your vocal warm-up, and definitely before any live performance or recording session. As you gain confidence and begin to believe in this true version of yourself, you will likely find more things to love about your artistry. Add them to the list. Meditate on it. I mean this quite literally. As a part of your daily work to untie your own emotional knots, you should take five minutes every day to clear your mind and set your positive intentions for the day ahead. If you are new to meditating and even if you are not, here is a **Mindful Breathing** exercise that I give to all of my clients, and especially those dealing with vocal dysphonia.

Sit cross-legged on the floor, or comfortably upright in a chair. If you're seated on a chair your legs should ideally be uncrossed. Rest your hands on your thighs, facing up. Close your eyes and take a full breath in through your nose to the count of four. Hold this breath to a count of seven, and then release all the air from your lungs to a count of eight. Repeat these steps five times, slowly and with positive intention. Your heart rate will regulate, your blood pressure will lower, your mind will have more clarity, and you will feel more grounded and present. This is a basic mindful breathing technique that is especially beneficial for singers. The goal is to reconnect you with what you love most about singing and to push away all the negative baggage that has piled up over the years.

If you commit to doing these two suggestions daily, you will eventually start to feel like you are making progress towards your goal. But the work doesn't stop there. Just like you don't stop doing your warm-ups when you reach your vocal goals, you shouldn't stop working on your emotional journey, just because you have a breakthrough. Your old demons will be only too happy to find a weakness to exploit, and as those of us with emotional triggers can attest, one, even unintentional, negative reaction can send us spiralling back down the rabbit hole. Positive affirmations and mindful breathing are a lifelong practice that should be embraced as a gift you give yourself every day.

BEHIND THE SCENES: LETTING GO OF SELF-DOUBT

Not all singers who suffer from vocal dysphonia as a result of negative emotional blocks are as difficult to rehabilitate as **Anon**. **Incog** came to see me for a similar issue. Her vocal dysphonia had not had as much time to take root, so we were able to rehab her voice and reset her emotional story in only a few short months. **Incog** had been the lead singer in a very popular band and was making the rough transition from teen heart-throb to adult rock star. This is not a shift that is easily made; many have not been able to make the leap.

I first met **Incog** when I was invited to sit in on a rehearsal for her upcoming tour. When I arrived at the rehearsal space, **Incog** was already on the stage. Her management invited me in because she was having some difficulty with her vocals. She had a strong sense of loyalty to her regular vocal coach, but she was also aware of the lack of progress in addressing her persistent problem. I sat through an hour of rehearsal and listened closely to every note. **Incog** had an incredible tone to her voice, but she was struggling with her Mix voice. I took notes on the key problems that I was able to identify, and we parted ways with a promise to reconnect some weeks later, when her tour brought her back to Los Angeles. It was almost a month later when I received another call from her management team. **Incog** was back in town, ready to try a few sessions with me.

When **Incog** walked into my studio, she presented a calm façade. In spite of her best, and admittedly very good efforts to mask the truth, I could tell that she was terrified. From my years of coaching singers, I could see from behind her eyes that her brain was running at one hundred miles an hour. Who could blame her? She was in a room with a virtual stranger waiting to hear the verdict on what was wrong with her voice. I assured her I was not there to judge, only to collaborate, help, and support. So we began to sing. She had the same, cool tone I heard during rehearsal, but singing the arpeggio warm-ups were immediately a challenge. Finding out you cannot sing a simple scale, in the middle of a successful career, is humbling, to say the least. **Incog** was no exception. Making matters worse, was an obvious, and debilitating undercurrent of self-doubt.

At this point, I knew that getting through to her on a personal level was more important than persisting with the technical work. So we stopped the scales and talked instead. Many times I will hear from my clients that a session with me is equal parts vocal coaching and therapy. This is deliberate on my part. I know that the only way to get the best out of my clients is to help them through their emotional difficulties, as much as their physical ones. She talked about her success that had come fast and furious. She had made a lot of money, was incredibly famous, and was now terrified that she could be washed up. **Incog** was afraid that she might never write another hit song or make money singing again. This is a persistent and common fear among artists.

Incog did not have a lot of self-love, and she was very hard on herself. When we ran through the arpeggios, she would continually stop and berate herself for falling short of her unrealistically high bar. I had to coach her through this, encouraging her to let go of the judgement, and to instead, push through like an athlete. Our sessions went on like this for several weeks. With each session, I gained a little more of her trust, and she regained more of her confidence. **Incog** also tackled her daily practice of positive affirmations and mindful breathing with surprising diligence.

Once she quieted the self-doubt and began to believe in herself again, she started to focus on what she wanted to build, instead of tearing herself down. At about the six month mark, **Incog** came into the studio having written a breakthrough hit song. I could tell it was a hit from the first listen. Sure enough, it went on to top charts, go platinum, and win multiple awards. She was well on her way to achieving everything she didn't think possible, only a few short months before. Her vocals were strong, and most important, she was loving the process *and herself* again.

SOCIAL MEDIA

Incog and **Anon** both feared the judgement of others, even though they were arguably their own worst critics. This leads me to the thing that has become a constant source of judgement for my clients, especially those from the millennial generation and younger.

It is social media, and it is causing our artists young and old, no end of stress and anxiety. Social media platforms are full of polished highlights, showing the world the best of our lives. Rarely will someone willingly present themselves as a flawed human being. I have often heard people call social media *soul killing*. And what is an artist without their soulfulness? How do we find the freedom to create, with its necessary failures and trips along the way when we are expected to share every moment of our day with a more often than not, judgmental audience?

I have seen the music industry change dramatically over the past few years, by making the number one measure of talent the artist's social media following and engagement. I have seen wildly talented artists, who ten years ago would have been at the center of a record label bidding war, not even considered today because of a weak Instagram following. This has meant that social media has become a necessary evil. The challenge is to approach social media with a healthy dose of humor to see how *you* can use *it* for good, rather than allowing *it* to use *you*. Use your positive affirmations and mindful breathing tools to make sure you make your mark without letting social media leave a mark on you.

Here's a fun challenge I give many of my clients who are struggling with social media running their lives. Do something amazing; take photos if you want, but don't post about it on social media. Instead, go out to lunch with a friend, talk about your experience, then show them the photos. Laugh, cry, and make connections with people in person.

Share your truth and listen to theirs.

MANTRAS/BREATHING

In addition to positive affirmations and mindful breathing, my clients have often found it helpful to incorporate **mantras**. Mantras take positive affirmations to the next level, and they are a powerfully effective tool at combating insecurities. You can write your own as the situation requires. Something simple like, *"I am not my Instagram. My social media status does not define me."* Or you could adopt something more universal, like this one I learned from a talented healer. *"I am surrounded by a forcefield and nothing and no one that does not serve me can enter."* I have seen the power of visualization help some of my most successful clients, and I have used this particular mantra effectively, many times in my own life.

For many of us, singing is our life as well as our life's work. Taking the time to work on your emotional journey alongside your vocal training, will give you the freedom to be creative and explore your artistry. Not only will your singing improve, but so will your overall sense of well-being and self-love. Keep at it, stay positive, re-visit your warm-up exercises, and see if you can feel the difference.

Don't forget to Breathe!!! There are many guided breathing tools online to help slow your heart rate down, lower your blood pressure and bring cortisol levels down. High cortisol levels cause high blood pressure, muscle weakness, anxiety and depression just to name a few. Breathing mindfully for five to 10 minutes each day will help alleviate these symptoms.

Stress is real for many people and can make you physically sick especially when you put a lot of pressure on yourself or have perfectionism and performance anxiety. Many of my artists experience stress and anxiety on tour. The stress is not just from the pressure of having to perform night after night, but dealing with other people around them constantly. Sleeping in different places most nights can also throw us off our schedules and send our bodies into major imbalance.

Mantras, breathing exercises, and proper sleep patterns are very important in our daily lives, but especially for folks who travel a lot, or tour, with pressures of performance.

TAKING CARE OF YOUR VOICE: PART 2
YOUR BODY

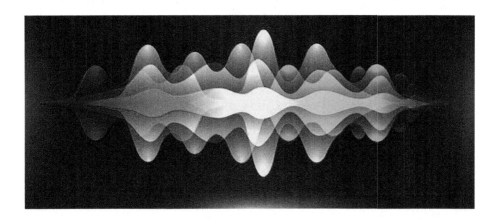

"After working with Valerie when I was on the show, 'Lucifer', I started to pay a lot more attention to both my vocal and physical fitness. She helped me realize that being a singer is like being an athlete."

—Tom Ellis, Actor

I n today's busy world, sometimes we need a reminder to prioritize our health. Good health supports a good life, and in turn, a successful career as a singer. We have to focus on our health in order to sing well and consistently over time, because being a professional singer is taxing. We push ourselves to our mental and physical limits in order to reach audiences with our unique stories. The health-related dangers of life on the road have been documented in many international movies and documentaries, from the Jim Morrison biopic "The Doors" to Oscar nominated "Straight Outta Compton". Much of the media attention centered around the life of a rock star emphasizes, and even encourages, unhealthy lifestyle choices. There are very few roadmaps out there to help singers along a nourishing path, both physically and emotionally.

Working directly with the world's best voice doctors, I have seen how poor physical health can dramatically affect a singer's voice over time. Whether I notice one of my clients is struggling, or if they are excelling and want to take their game to the next level, I will take time during our sessions to focus on nutrition and exercise. Vocal, mental, and physical health need to be kept in check, and if any of them are noticeably out of balance, your success and confidence as a singer will deteriorate. Through navigating my own health crises, I have worked with many nutritionists, fitness trainers, and doctors— Eastern and Western, and I am committed to passing on the tools I have learned. I think it's imperative to highlight some of the potential health-related pitfalls in the life of a singer, the challenges of combating them, and the simple tools you can implement to come out on top.

PITFALLS ON TOUR

During tours, sleeping and diet are usually the first things to be put on the back burner *or forgotten altogether*. Burgers, fries, and other heavy, greasy foods on the road, will make you feel bloated and tired, and if you are overloading your body with sugar from late night snacking and drinking alcohol, you are also going to compromise your immune system. You may find that you are getting sick more often and generally feeling exhausted.

Anxiety is also a leading cause of sickness, because it fires too much of the stress hormone, cortisol, into the brain, which is absolutely toxic.

Taking sleeping pills, antibiotics, steroids, and other medications to counteract these pitfalls, usually just masks the underlying issues.

BEHIND THE SCENES: LOSING FOCUS

One of my hardest working clients is the frontman for a chart-topping band. The band tours the world, packing stadiums from Shanghai to Vienna. They are committed to their craft and at the start of their tours, they are fiercely focused. Not surprisingly, the first performances go spectacularly well. But after checking off a few successful shows, things relax a little and the band starts to lose their focus and push the limits. One night in particular stands out in my mind.

A few days before, their girlfriends and a couple of close friends had joined them on the tour. Their after-show parties were extending into the early morning hours—drinking, smoking, etc. The partying carried on through the night, which happened to be the night before a very important show that was to be attended by representatives from their label. When it was time for them to hit the stage the next night, they were physically drained. On stage, their voices were strained and their energies forced. They did not perform at the level they were more than capable of achieving. It was the *worst* show of the entire tour.

The group felt disappointed and disheartened. It was a wake-up call to correct their destructive behavior. Sometimes on tour, I find myself in the position to be a voice of reason, so I took this opportunity to step forward and suggest that the band might consider taking advantage of the three-day break in their tour schedule to lay low for a few days. No partying, no drinking, no late nights; just rest and regroup. They followed my suggestion, and their commitment to self-care over the next three days resulted in a show that was unparalleled. They came back strong and crushed it.

YOUR TURN: PERFORMANCE DAYS

On performance days on the road or at home, I recommend refraining from eating a full meal at least two hours before showtime, to avoid an upset stomach and to help you feel light and energized. It is no fun trying to perform while at the same time digesting a full serving of pasta with cream sauce. If you feel hungry in the hours leading up to a performance, try to stick to light snacks like nuts and fresh fruits and vegetables. Then, right before showtime, sip a cup of decaffeinated tea, with a teaspoon of Manuka honey. This extraordinary honey is a little harder to find and also a bit more expensive, but it delivers a powerful antioxidant punch, as well as providing a protective coating for the throat. If you find that dairy makes your body produce more mucus, then avoid dairy products on show day, all together. The goal is to help you feel light and energetic on the stage. Always use your common sense, avoid foods you know create imbalance in your body, and when in doubt, consult your doctor or nutritionist.

MAINTAINING DAILY PHYSICAL HEALTH

The stressors of touring are real. Stealing sleep where you can on buses and in airports, while maintaining a head-spinning schedule of press and show dates, with pre and post-show meet and greets is no easy task. It is no wonder artists look for relief wherever they can. Temptations are everywhere for rock stars, and it takes a tremendous will to avoid them night after night. We all face temptations every day; they may not seem as intoxicating as those offered to a rock star, but each one of us has to make decisions every day to avoid them. Side-stepping processed foods, staying up too late or too much alcohol, in favor of fresh fruits and vegetables, to drinking eight glasses of water a day, exercise, and six to eight hours of shut-eye, takes commitment. These are exactly the same choices faced by the touring vocal artist. At its core, taking care of yourself as a singer is pretty straightforward. But there are specific ways to strategize your diet and daily routine in order to position your health for the challenges you will face on the road or in the studio.

SLEEP

Health is my highest currency, so sleep is my highest priority, and I am always talking to my clients about the importance of it. Just because many of my singers on the road are still in their teenage years and twenties, does not mean they do not need have a full night's sleep or short naps during the day. No matter what age you are, if you are dealing with a crazy schedule, try taking a power nap to balance life on the road or at home. It makes a big difference, and every time I see a singer for a session *after a nap,* they look more refreshed and feel better. Many of my artists take prescription sleeping aids. I usually suggest they discuss with an Eastern doctor more natural, homeopathic remedies, incorporating meditation techniques to still their mind and body. It can take time to wean themselves off their 'comfort blankets'. One of the biggest hurdles with singers is talking to them about healthier ways to relax and sleep, rather than taking Valium and various sleeping pills. Prescription sleeping medication can be a slippery slope.

DIET

I recommend diets that do not require any extremes, but rather a thoughtful shift toward eating habits where you minimize your intake of carbohydrates and sugars, which sap your energy. Processed food and sugar can have serious negative effects on your overall health. Instead, work on getting your protein from unprocessed, natural sources, and fresh vegetables. Choose foods that are fresh. If it is in a can, box, or wrapped in plastic, it should account for a very small percentage of your overall caloric intake. Sounds pretty simple, but with the schedules we keep and easy access to fast food on the road, it can be surprisingly difficult to implement.

WATER

Then there is water… the importance of which cannot be over-stated. Our bodies are made up of sixty to seventy percent water, and if you do not drink plenty of it, your energy will lag and you may even feel depressed and unmotivated. Dehydration wreaks havoc on your SPA and every other system in your body. The right amount of water to drink every day is different for each of us, but if you are a healthy adult you should aim for a minimum of sixty-four to eighty ounces a day. Some of my clients, who are on a high-octane work-out program, or rehearsal and tour schedule, down a full gallon daily, but this will feel like far too much for many of us, and it probably is. There are a number of factors to consider when determining how much

H2O you need daily to achieve optimal health, including the climate in which you live, your weight, and your activity level. There are a number of on-line calculators to help you narrow down how much water you need. I like to squeeze a little fresh lemon in my glass of water to make it more appetizing, along with a boost of Vitamin C.

SUPPLEMENTS

Because of the pollution in our air and lack of nutrients in our food, I encourage discussing with a nutritionist using dietary supplements, including a plant-based Vitamin C, Vitamin B, Probiotics, and the antioxidant, Glutathione. When you are sick or your immune system is compromised, Echinacea, Oregano Oil, Olive Leaf, and Colloidal Silver can be great boosters. Which supplements, and how much or how little you take of each, is a decision between you, your body, and your doctor or nutritionist.

BEHIND THE SCENES: DEALING WITH SICKNESS

In spite of best efforts, clients do sometimes fall ill. One of my clients fell sick on tour right before a major performance. He had been touring for weeks, and the combination of his lack of sleep and not-so-infrequent dietary lapses, had compromised his immune system. He had been diligent in keeping up his vocal warm-up routine, so his voice was still strong, and he felt it was essential for him to get through this performance. Instead of turning to prescription drugs, I discussed with his doctor, and we recommended he have one of the tour's day runners call in a local nurse to administer a Myer's Cocktail IV drip. It contains a potent combination of vitamins, including C and B12, and minerals including Magnesium, which can help to immediately boost energy and expedite healing. It is not uncommon for artists to use these drips on the road as a way of enhancing their overall wellness and to keep their immune systems in peak condition.

If you, like most of us, do not have a private nurse on standby with a Myer's drip, you can still up your vitamin intake, and keep yourself rested and hydrated. I respect and value Western medicine, but I am also an advocate of Eastern approaches to health and wellness, which focus on natural remedies. Prescription drugs have their place, but they should not be the first thing on your mind every time you fall ill.

I want to briefly touch on the issue of the overuse of prescription medicines. On my roster, I have clients who are constantly on rounds of steroids and antibiotics for various health issues, which may or may not be improving their overall wellness. What is clear is that these prescriptions are weakening their guts. Over fifteen years of getting my own gut in check, I have learned that the gut is the central part of our immune system and overall health. If it is weakened by too many painkillers, antibiotics, steroids, bad food, and more, we will not have enough good bacteria in the stomach, which leaves us with a weakened immune system. This can lead to other health issues and create serious roadblocks on your path to becoming the best singer you can be.

BEHIND THE SCENES: MYSTERY SICKNESS

Another client of mine who is a talented session singer and musician, had his livelihood impacted by a poorly managed health issue. ◊ was, by all accounts, very fit, and took pretty good care of himself. Singing in nightclubs and studio sessions was his bread and butter. He didn't have a publishing deal or any record sales, so if he wasn't on stage or in the studio singing, he wasn't getting paid.

He came to me with vocal issues, which I initially identified as over-singing, caused in part by acid reflux. After speaking with him about his diet, I couldn't immediately identify the possible source of the acid reflux. I recommended he visit a voice doctor to rule out any issues with his SPA. The scope showed a little redness and swelling, but nothing that warranted treatment. Still, as ◊ and I worked together, his problems persisted, so we sought a second opinion. The diagnosis was the same. A little redness and swelling, but nothing they could clearly identify or treat.

We went on like this for a few weeks, and I did what I could to help him work around his mysterious acid reflux, until one day, ◊ walked into my studio looking particularly unwell. I had seen this look before... *in myself.* He sat down exhausted, his eyes bloodshot. His physical issues had gotten substantially worse. He had developed a rash all over his body, and he looked completely depleted. He told me he felt like he was dying. He knew it couldn't be the case, but he had never felt so unwell in his life. He knew something was very, very wrong, and his doctors said they couldn't find the cause.

We tried again to get to the bottom of the mystery. We considered his acid reflux again, which sparked a conversation about Candida, which he admitted was something he had battled for a long time. Candida is a yeast, and we all have a certain amount of it in our bodies, but when we experience imbalance in our gut, the yeast can overgrow, causing all manner of health problems. Stress, poor nutrition, and prescription medicines are a handful of things that can lead to this imbalance.

I have battled with Candida many times, and he was exhibiting all the classic symptoms I have experienced, too. It is brutal, but can be addressed, if you know where to look, and what to do. I asked him again about his diet, and he was still eating all the right things, so I dug a little further. I revealed that in addition to over the counter acid reflux pills, he was taking four different medications, all prescribed by the doctors who had admitted to not knowing exactly what the problem was that they were trying to treat. Rather than sending him home empty handed, between the two of them, they had prescribed antibiotics, steroids and anti-fungal meds. These, had each in turn exacerbated his Candida overgrowth, which had fueled his acid reflux, further hurting his voice.

This was a classic case of someone whose non-vocal health issue, in his case, a gut disorder, and anxiety was negatively impacting his work and performance. He didn't know the acid reflux was coming from the Candida, and in a misguided effort to self-medicate, he was taking over-the-counter acid reflux meds by the barrelful, which blocked his natural stomach acids, only adding to his gut imbalance and Candida overgrowth. Adding in all the prescription medicines only made matters worse.

I sent him to my amazing Eastern doctor for supplemental help, and then I recommended he commit to two weeks of complete vocal rest and meditation to give his body a chance to recover. This was a terrifying proposition for a musician who lives paycheck to paycheck, performance to performance, but it was the only way to get his body back in balance, so he could get back to feeling and singing his best. His sacrifice paid off, and he now has a balanced gut, a healthy voice, and a long career ahead of him.

BE YOUR OWN ADVOCATE

I want to make it clear that I am not trying to demonize prescription drugs or Western medicine. They have helped me many times in my life and, no doubt, will again. What I do want to get across, however, is the importance of communicating; letting your doctor know what medications you are on or have tried (prescription and over-the-counter), what supplements you are taking, and all known health issues, even if they don't seem to be related to your current complaint. Ask questions and demand a deeper look into your issues. You need to be your own advocate for your healthcare. Your voice, and your livelihood, depend on it.

EXERCISE

I use so many athletic analogies in my teaching and in this book because I have been athletic my entire life, from competing as a gymnast and playing five years of soccer, to running track in high school and teaching aerobic classes. Physical fitness has always been a priority for me.

For many artists, performing on stage can be a workout. If your stage routine includes dancing and high energy running and jumping, then you will find your performances and your stamina are improved with regular workouts. Injuries, like strained leg muscles and pulled back muscles, are not uncommon among rock and pop singers. Taking the time to work out your body and strengthen your core, is as important as warming up your vocal cord muscles. If you haven't exercised much before, or are scared of the machines in the gym and do not know where to start, hiring a trainer for a couple of sessions, or asking a friend for guidance, can help set you on the right path. Of course, don't forget to check in with your chosen health care professionals before starting a new exercise routine.

If you are already feeling pain in your body from the repetitive strain of on-stage leaps and across-stage runs, chiropractic adjustments and physical therapy, combined with massage and acupuncture, can be a recommended route before launching into a work-out routine.

One of my clients had a choreographed show that had him running up a set of stairs, jumping off monitors and drum kits, all while singing through his intense setlist. He was only in his twenties, but all that leaping left him with painful legs and knees. His trainer had him use tension bands to strengthen his joints and thighs, then added massage into his routine to keep his muscles loose. He worked through these exercises daily, even up until hours before the show while in his dressing room. Not only did his pain go away, but his agility and stamina on stage increased.

There are lower cost, equally effective alternatives to hiring a personal trainer and massage therapist. Go for a run, lift weights, stretch and strengthen your body through yoga and pilates—there are many fitness videos on YouTube to help you get started. Find what works, stick with it, and then mix it up again. As you increase your cardiovascular fitness, you will feel an increased capacity to sing with openness and clarity. Exercise opens up your lungs, so much so, that many of my clients exercise before a session with me so they can take full advantage of our time together.

Whether you are spending a lot of time in rehearsals, sound checks, on a bus, in a plane, or just dreaming of a time when you will be, you must prioritize your physical health. Proper nutrition and exercise will help support your efforts to excel as a singer. You will feel better, your body will be more responsive, and your immune system will be able to fight off sickness more effectively. Because the music business has changed so much over the last several years, artists are asked to do more and give more of themselves. To survive and thrive in this world, you have to look after and manage your vocal, mental, and physical health.

THE PRESSURE OF PERFECTION
& TELLING YOUR TRUTH

"Working with Val has been fantastic! Her warm-ups and dedicated exercises are amazing and get me ready to rumble! To have her on the side-lines, listening and helping to make me a better singer has been invaluable. Val is a blessing! She's an incredible talent, and I'm thankful for her instruction and her drive to take me to another level!"

—Gary LeVox, *Rascall Flatts*

Singers are storytellers. Without their voices, they lose the ability to communicate those stories, *their truth*, with the world. This is why I devote my time to teaching singers arpeggios and how their SPA works; why I spend hours upon hours every week helping singers expand their range and stamina; why I take time away from my family to travel with a band on tour. I want singers to find their authentic voice, to know how their instrument works, so they can have a long and impactful career.

Arpeggios are not hit songs, they are not ground-breaking or award-winning, but they are the foundation to building a career as a professional singer. More often than not, when a new client walks through my door, they want to jump into their music. They are excited for me to show them how to sing that high note they have been struggling with, or give them the stamina they need to last through a set. When I start playing a scale, I often see the disappointment in their eyes. It's true... scales are boring! I will be the first to admit it. I play thousands of them every single week. As the singer begrudgingly works through that first lip roll and follows my directions to make small adjustments to their sound, I love that moment when their eyes light up, as they realize they are easily singing the notes they were struggling with. We go on to build on that first exercise with more difficult ones that are specific for their vocal personality, and only then we can start the fun part of incorporating the tools they just learned into their songs.

Lack of range and stamina are the two main issues singers come to me to resolve. The most frustrating part of this for many singers, is that it limits what songs they can write. Their stories are being short-changed, or have to be given to other artists, because they do not possess the tools to be able to sing them as they should be sung or written. One way around decreased range and stamina that some artists end up utilizing, is to get a 'perfect take' in the recording studio, often with the aid of auto-tune and heavy mixing. They then rely on that recording in live performance—usually combined with lowering the key of the song. While this is an option, what I have discovered are these solutions create a crutch, destroying the singer's confidence on stage over time, impairing their freedom to share their story with an audience. What is frustrating for me, is how easy these issues can be fixed with just a little bit of proper coaching and focused practice.

I have watched the music industry change over the past three decades, and the expectation of perfection in both recording and live performances is growing... it's not going away any time soon. This shift means that it is more and more difficult for singers to share their authentic voice and tell their truth. Audiences now **expect** to hear their favorite artists' live performances sound **exactly** like the recording. Labels and managers feel the pressure to purchase expensive, top of the line, live audio tuning equipment. This equipment creates its own problems, as the singer starts to experience even more stress and anxiety, because they feel fake, since they cannot sing their own songs live without rigs and auto-tune. The more auto-tune has to be used, the less authentic the voice sounds. Although that electronic sound is preferred in a few genres, it does not mean the singer shouldn't learn to sing on pitch in a live setting. If singers learn and implement the tools to make their voices bionic and authentic, they do not have to rely on equipment to give their fans the performance of a lifetime, night after night. Singers should have the confidence to go on stage and know their voices will be there for them. Audiences will continue to expect perfection, but hopefully, over time, they will grow to enjoy the perfectly imperfect experience of live performances—just like we cherish the live, raw, analog recordings of The Eagles, Journey, The Beatles, Prince, Tears for Fears, and many more.

The pressure of perfection versus authenticity spills over into all areas of music. While working on a film project, I spoke with the vice-president of music supervision for one of the top film production companies in America. Our discussion about vocal sessions for an academy award winning actor quickly moved onto the reason why training this actor's singing voice for the part, was as important as her studying the character she would be portraying. For both of us, the driving force was being authentic to the story and person the story was based on. If the singing was off, the whole scene would not work.

He told me about his experience of working on *Bohemian Rhapsody*, which used all of Freddie Mercury's tracks from the original *Queen* recordings. At one point, the project almost came to a screeching halt. If you have watched the movie, there is a pivotal scene outside the club where Freddie auditions for the band. The problem occurred when they could not find any recordings of Freddie singing that song *a cappella,* and that moment needed to sound just as authentic as the rest of the movie. After a global search, they found a singer in Nashville who could mimic Freddie's voice perfectly, and saved the movie. Whether it is on a stage, record, or movie, telling the truth with the singer's voice is essential, and that is why knowing your voice, and how it works, is so important to you telling your story as a singer.

I worked with an artist who was about to embark on a five-month tour, opening for two other Grammy award-winning artists. My client could really sing. After several weeks of sessions at my studio, I came to the last rehearsal. With my 'in-ears' in, I listened to the entire set with the mix the audience would be hearing— auto-tune, stacked background vocals, super loud tracks with a lot of reverb. I have to say... I was bored. It felt as if they could have almost placed a cardboard cut-out of him on stage and hit 'play' on his album. I know that may sound harsh, but that's how I heard the show. I asked his engineer and my client about it, and they said his management wanted the tracks loud, with a ton of background vocals in the mix, because the head-liners had that. They were afraid their client's performance would not match the other band's perfection in large stadiums. On the next run through, I asked the engineer to turn off the auto-tune, then turn down all the tracks and background vocals. My client agreed and began to sing the set. It was magic! I saw him come to life and sing more precisely. He sounded amazing. I felt goosebumps. Instead of sounding computerized, his performance was electric! Sure, as he moved around on stage, there were a few notes here and there that were not pitch perfect, but wow, it was great to listen to and watch. My client and I knew his management would probably still want the big sound, so he said he would discuss with them, the idea of splitting the difference. He had more fun the second run though, because he felt his voice, *his truth,* being heard.

Using my method has another benefit besides increased range, stamina and authenticity. It also helps singers to avoid vocal injuries by maintaining healthy voice. As a coach, I can show my clients what they need to do, giving them all the tools, but it takes them believing in themselves and putting in the hard work to achieve vocal freedom. *"Vocal Health for Life"* has been my mantra for years, and everything I teach is guided by that phrase. Some artists come to me with an established career tied to a signature sound that is actually harming their voice, so our focus becomes how to recreate that same sound in a healthy way. The SPA is far more complex and flexible than we give it credit for. Sometimes it takes quite a bit of experimentation, but we always figure out how to sing their songs in a healthy way without sacrificing their sound.

YOUR TURN: WHAT THIS MEANS FOR YOU

Many singers believe the voice they were born with is their beginning, middle, and end. I was chatting with a new client after their first session, and they said, "I didn't realize so much went into singing, I thought it was something that you are just born with, or not." Imagine a lead guitarist or drummer getting up on stage with little to no training or practice. The show would fall apart and they would be fired. As a singer, you should put the same demand on yourself to learn your instrument as much as the rest of the band. An instrument is an instrument whether it is part of your body or bought from a store. You can be bionic.

If you want to commit to this path, start by using the insights I have shared here to find your baseline. Be honest with yourself and your voice. It is okay if you have been singing for years and realize you feel like you need to start over. *Commit to the process, not the outcome.* The journey is the longest part, and if you only focus on where you want to be, you will miss out on the important lessons along the way. Take fifteen minutes a day to sing through arpeggios designed for your vocal personality and you will soon realize, like many of my artists, that you cannot believe you used to go on stage or record a song without warming up properly.

Your singing journey needs to continue beyond this book. Once you have found out your baseline, translate the knowledge you have learned into finding the right vocal coach for you. Just because someone has a great client roster, does not automatically make them a great teacher. Highlight the sections in this book that speak to you, so you can ask educated questions as you start seeking out someone who can take your voice to the next level. At my studio, my team of vocal coaches and I, help clients find their authentic voice. If you have questions, do not be afraid to contact us. In fact, I encourage you to reach out and let us know about your voice and goals.

Please be sure to avail of my Master Classes in vocal training, found via the link provided for a free month with **Skillshare**. The Master Classes are a start to finish, in-depth discussion about singing, vocal anatomy, *how to's*, and the music industry, today. With the help of one of my amazing clients, each class is like being in a one on one session with me, and is geared for beginners through advanced singers. We have also created a discount code for the **bettervoice.co** vocal trainer that I use with all of my clients. We have stream-lined a tried and true method by creating a simple, durable and invaluable tool that takes the classic straw exercises to a new level, and is a must have, no matter where you are on your personal journey to *a better voice*.

Let me leave you with this: *surround yourself with people who are smarter than you and always be open to asking for help. You have the opportunity to share your truth with the world, so take the time to discover how your voice works. Give your story the voice it deserves.*

—Val

Epilogue

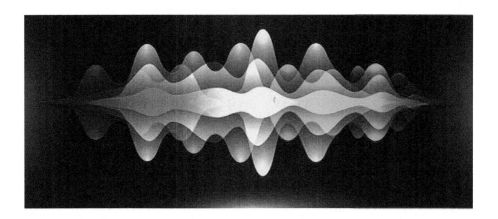

As I was on tour with Sam Smith in March and April of 2023, this book was heading off to print when I realized that I had left out some individuals who use their voices constantly and are very important in the fabric of our world's tapestry.

I was speaking to Sam's head of security, who served twenty-four years in the British military. In the midst of a casual conversation one day, something he said reminded me of the fact that many branches of the military could use classes on how to use their voices properly in cadence and drills.

Cadence is traditional call and response work sung by military personnel while running/marching. It is a modulation or inflection in the voice that contains a musical phrase. Cadence ensures that the troops are in formation and keep time. Cadence synchronizes breathing and helps with fitness. However, if someone is calling/answering cadence and they are not breathing properly while running, it could result in tired or swollen vocal cords and lost voices.

I then remembered when my own brother (who was in the Marine Corps for eight years), became a drill instructor at Camp Pendleton in Oceanside, California. He trained young marines and ran them through cadence in boot camp to prepare for whatever they would face in their time with the military. My brother, Steve, would lose his voice constantly. I remember a former boyfriend of mine who faced the same dilemma when he headed into the Marine Corps, just a year after my brother.

Proper vocal warm-up isn't just for the entertainment industry. As we see from the story above, warming up the voice before placing demands such as call and response, could save so many people the hassle of vocal strain or damage. My book editor, Mary Helen, is a Doctor of Chiropractic and public speaker who talks to people all day long, six days a week. She runs through my vocal warm-ups in the shower and while getting ready for work each morning. She even uses the Better Voice Vocal Trainer as she drives to work and says it's just as important in her daily routine as warming up and stretching before she adjusts spines throughout her work day.

There is no one who uses their voice for extended or intense periods of time who doesn't benefit from targeted exercises and proper vocal training.

EPILOGUE

We are so looking forward to starting work on the follow-up to this book. Now that you know the story of how my life's work has centered around helping my clients achieve a better voice, our next adventure will be a multi-media conceptual book, using the written word, audio and video to take your vocal skills to the next level.

Dr. Mary Helen Hensley is an expert in the fields of neuroscience and metaphysics. We will be combining our knowledge of physical, emotional and energetic health and well-being, to create a book that will offer a unique and immersive adventure for those who want to achieve a healthy and fulfilling vocal experience.

Valerie Morehouse is the go-to vocal coach in the entertainment business today. Valerie earned a B.F.A in Journalism and was one of the youngest students at Chapman University to earn a spot in the acclaimed Chamber Singers, led by Dr. William Hall. The program is one of the most rigorous voice departments at the colligate level.

Valerie has worked alongside the world's top ear, nose, and throat surgeons to develop a methodology to rehabilitate singers at warp speed from vocal misuse and trauma. Valerie's method not only increases the singer's range and technical ability, but also keeps the voice healthy while maintaining the singer's signature sound. Working hand in hand with doctors at the forefront of their field to rehabilitate clients who suffer from nodules, polyps, paralyzed cords, and vocal dysphonia, Valerie has given new hope to clients who faced the possibility they may never recover.

Valerie's journey started about thirty years ago when she was diagnosed with debilitating nodules on her vocal cords. Having sung all her life, the idea of not being able to sing again was not an option.

She devoted herself to finding out what causes vocal trauma and how to prevent it. For over two decades, Valerie's personal mission of **Vocal Health For Life** has transformed the lives of many successful artists working today, including: Reeve Carney, Sam Smith, Christina Perri, Olivia Rodrigo, The Chainsmokers, Sia, 5SOS, Britney Spears, Jeff Bridges, and Noah Cyrus, just to name a few. She also prepares actors' voices for stage, television, and film, including Jessica Chastain (The Eyes of Tammy Faye), Sally Hawkins (The Shape of Water), Tom Ellis (Lucifer), the cast of Nashville (ABC & CMT), and FOX sportscaster, Joe Buck.

In January 2019, Valerie launched her podcast, LipRoll, on all platforms, featuring conversations with her clients and key industry players—the show gives an inside look into the entertainment industry and the struggles and highlights they all encounter. In 2021, Valerie partnered with the Better Voice Company, introducing the best vocal training device she has ever seen, helping clients reach their potential with rapid results.

From her studio in Los Angeles, Valerie mentors and coaches singers all around the world by giving them the tools to avoid vocal issues down the road and to be prepared for the rigors of touring and recording.

Better Voice Vocal Trainer

The Vocal Trainer by Better Voice is backed by the science of SOVT Exercises. SOVT stands for Semi-Occluded Vocal Tract. These exercises limit the amount of acoustic air pressure that can escape from your mouth while vocalising.

- Expand your range
- Eliminate voices cracks
- Gain exceptional control
- Make singing effortless
- Reduce tension/tightness

Jada Wedding: BA (Hons) Musical Theatre Performance Student
International College of Musical Theatre - London

Use BVVT10 at checkout for 10% off the Better Voice Vocal Trainer at

www.bettervoice.store

SKILL™ SHare.

Skillshare is the world's largest online learning platform for creativity. On Skillshare, members can choose from tens of thousands of interactive and engaging classes in everything from graphic design to photography, painting, illustration, interior design, music, and more, all taught by leading industry experts. Members become a part of a vibrant community of professionals and new learners alike, all eager to get inspired and grow their skillset by tapping into their creativity.

Check out Skillshare for yourself – you can even start with Val's class on vocal training! Use the QR code or link below to enjoy one free month of Skillshare.

www.skillshare.com

Use Valerie's discount code at

http://skl.sh/valerie-morehouse

The Ultimate Theatre Education Experience

We inspire, empower and challenge aspiring performing artists to hone their craft through online masterclasses with top Broadway and West End talent.

Be sure to visit Valerie's page at

www.boommasterclass.com

Use BOOM10 at checkout for 10% off BOOM membership and purchases

Acknowledgements

My heartfelt thanks to my family, staff and friends for all of their love and support throughout this project. A special thanks to Amanda Luttrell Garrigus for helping me to organize my thoughts into content, and to Dr. Mary Helen Hensley and Book Hub Publishing for editing and bringing "A Better Voice" to life.